The Queen's Own Hussars

The Colonel-in-Chief *John Gilroy*
From a painting in the Officers' Mess

Dedicated to Her Majesty Queen Elizabeth The Queen Mother
Colonel-in-Chief The Queen's Own Hussars
by the members of Her Regiment

The production of this book would not have been possible without the most generous grant from The British Reinforced Concrete Engineering Co. Ltd, of Stafford. Furthermore, the Company has agreed that any subsequent profits should be given entirely to Regimental Charities.

The Queen's Own Hussars

Tercentenary Edition

1685–1985

BRASSEY'S DEFENCE PUBLISHERS
A member of the Pergamon Group

LONDON * OXFORD * WASHINGTON D.C. * NEW YORK
TORONTO * SYDNEY * FRANKFURT

First published by
The Queen's Own Hussars, 28 Jury Street, Warwick, CV34 4EW

This edition published in 1985 by Brassey's Defence Publishers Ltd.,
a member of the Pergamon Group, Maxwell House,
74 Worship Street, London EC2A 2EN

Text copyright © The Queen's Own Hussars Regimental Museum 1985

All rights reserved. No part of this publication may be
reproduced, stored in a retrieval system, or transmitted,
in any form or by any means, electronic, mechanical,
photocopying, recording or otherwise, without the prior
permission in writing of The Queen's Own Hussars.

ISBN 0 08 033595 0

Printed and made in Great Britain at
The Roundwood Press, Kineton, Warwick

CONTENTS

List of Illustrations — 6

Foreword — 9

Chapter 1: A Short History — 10

Chapter 2: Battle Honours — 16

Chapter 3: More Recent History — 47

Chapter 4: The Famous–The Eccentric–The Unorthodox — 54

Chapter 5: Some Aspects of Regimental Life — 61

Chapter 6: Affiliations — 77

Chapter 7: Horse to Tank — 83

Chapter 8: Some Unusual Facts — 90

Chapter 9: Colonels and Commanding Officers since Amalgamation — 94

Bibliography — 95

LIST OF ILLUSTRATIONS

frontispiece

The Colonel-in-Chief

between pages 12 and 13

The First Colonel of the Regiment
Lieutenant-Colonel Charles Hagart
Thomas Brown regaining the lost Guidon
Stable Duty
Acquiring a "Seat"
The Passage of the Bidassoa

between pages 24 and 25

The 7th Hussars charging the French cavalry at Waterloo
Trenches kit
The Taking of Rifle Wood
The Marquess of Anglesey

between pages 36 and 37

3rd King's Own (Light) Dragoons, 1835
Victory at Beda Fomm

between pages 48 and 49

Personal maintenance
The Battle of Moodkee
The Light Camel Corps
The Battle of Chillianwallah
"A" Squadron, 3rd Hussars, 1936
Mk VI Light Tank
The 7th Hussars Drumhorse, 1876

between pages 60 and 61

Cornet Samuel Russell
The 7th Hussars Last Mounted Parade
The 7th Hussars First Mechanised Parade
"Boots and Saddle"

between pages 72 and 73

The First Regimental Polo Team
Armoured car patrol in Haifa
Armoured car patrol in Aden
Musical ride

between pages 84 and 85

The Suffolk Road Riot
Unloading horses, 1914
Loading tanks, 1960
Field Service Marching Order No 1

ACKNOWLEDGEMENTS

The authors of articles would like to acknowledge the help that they have received from the books listed in the Bibliography

EDITOR'S NOTE

In order to avoid confusion, the titles "3rd Hussars", "7th Hussars", and "Trooper" have been employed in some articles rather than the titles in use at the time.

FOREWORD

by Lieutenant-General Sir Robin Carnegie, KCB, OBE
Colonel of the Regiment

This book has been produced to celebrate our Tercentenary. It is not a conventional short history of The Queen's Own Hussars, but a series of articles written by members of the Regiment. I believe that together they give the unique character of The Queen's Own Hussars as it has developed over the last three hundred years.

I would like to take this opportunity to thank all those Queen's Own Hussars, serving and retired – well over a hundred – who have helped with the production of this book. I am particularly grateful to Brigadier James Rucker who in the early stages collected much of the material.

I hope that many who read this book will be encouraged to take a further interest in our great traditions, for not only is this study enjoyable in itself but these same traditions set the standards that we shall strive for in the future.

CHAPTER ONE

A Short History

by Lieutenant-Colonel D J M Jenkins
Commanding Officer

The Founding of the Regiments

In 1685 the Catholic King James II succeeded his brother Charles and almost immediately faced a rebellion from the Duke of Monmouth. This necessitated increasing the size of the army and thus Captains Leveson, Williams and Hussey were commissioned to raise troops of dragoons from the counties adjacent to London to guard the city. Following the defeat of Monmouth, three further troops were added to form The Queen Consorts Regiment of Dragoons under the Colonelcy of Charles Seymour Duke of Somerset. In 1688 William of Orange landed to claim the English throne which challenged the loyalty of James' army. The bulk of the Regiment turned to the Protestant William and after his succession, he gave the Colonelcy to Leveson. Following the custom of the time, the Regiment adopted the name of the Colonel and thus became Leveson's Dragoons. In 1689 they moved to Ireland to fight the army of James II and from 1689–1692 took part in many skirmishes, raids and actions including the Battle of the Boyne in 1690 which crushed James II's hopes.

William III also faced rebellion in Scotland where there was some hereditary loyalty to James. Regiments and troops of horses were raised from the Scottish gentry loyal to William and on 30 December 1689 Colonel Cunningham was ordered to assume command of a regiment of dragoons formed from some of these troops – this Regiment was established as Cunningham's Dragoons by February 1690. For the next two years the Regiment was engaged on peace keeping duties in Scotland.

Leveson's Dragoons returned from Ireland in 1692 and in 1694 both Leveson's and Cunningham's Dragoons were ordered to the Low Countries for their first engagement with the French. They took part in William's campaigns of 1694–1696 which were fought on the formalised lines of seventeenth-century warfare with sieges and raids but with no general engagement in which the cavalry could distinguish itself. Following peace in 1697 both Regiments returned to garrison duties in Britain.

Neither Regiment took part in Marlborough's magnificent victories against the French in the war of the Spanish succession 1702–1713 but The Queen Consort's Regiment took part in two campaigns against France's ally Spain. The first in 1702 involved an unsuccessful siege of Cadiz and a successful raid on Vigo in Spain and the second campaign in Spain in 1707–1708 included the Battle of Almensa in 1707. The Regiment withdrew in 1708 to return to garrison duty in

Britain. By 1709 the Colonelcy of Cunningham's had changed twice and in that year Ker assumed command. Ker's Dragoons joined the army in the Lowlands in 1712 but saw no action before peace was signed in 1713.

George I on his accession in 1714 changed the title of The Queen Consort's Regiment to the 3rd King's Own Regiment of Dragoons. The same year saw strong parliamentary objections to the cost of the army and so Ker's Dragoons were disbanded. However, the rebellion of James Stuart in Scotland in 1715 required an enlarged army and so Ker's Dragoons were reconstituted in 1715 and given the title of HRH The Princess of Wales' Own Royal Regiment of Dragoons. Both Regiments took part in the 1715 campaign against the Scots and the Battle of Sherifmuir. This led to the collapse of the rebellion and for the next 27 years the Regiments followed the normal nomadic life of the time. There were no barracks and so regiments moved round Britain billeted on the local population and recruiting where they could. Troops were normally billeted in separate towns and – as there was no police force – acted as an internal security force or a revenue force to prevent smuggling. On the accession of George II when there was no Princess of Wales, Ker's Dragoons were retitled The Queen's Own Regiment of Dragoons. The nomadic life of both Regiments came to an end in 1742 when they were ordered abroad to take part in the war of the Austrian Succession against the French.

The Wars against the French

The dragoon was originally intended to be a mounted infantryman and had to be prepared to fight on foot – a duty to which only lip service was paid by 1742. Dragoons were armed with musket and sword and rode horses of 15 to 15.2 hands in height. Orders issued in 1755 stated "no officer is supposed ever to fight himself any more than defend his head ... his business is to see his men fight and do well". The casualties suffered by officers in the French wars suggest lip service was paid to this too.

The first battle of the war occurred on 27 June 1743 at Dettingen when the English as part of an Allied Army soundly defeated the French. Both The King's Own and The Queen's Own Dragoons were heavily involved. The 3rd have special memories of the battle because of the bravery of Thomas Brown and the capture of the silver drums. Both Regiments fought at the next major engagement at Fontenoy in 1745 – though with less effect in what was a predominantly infantry battle.

Immediately after Fontenoy the 3rd were ordered back to England to face the rebellion of Bonnie Prince Charlie. They took part in the skirmish with the Prince's rear guard at Clifton Moor in 1745 and the battle of Culloden in 1746 which destroyed the Prince's army. The 3rd took no further part in the war with the French but The Queen's Own Dragoons fought at two further battles at Roucoux in 1746 and Val in 1747 before peace was signed in 1748.

In July 1751 George II signed a warrant numbering regiments in order of precedence and so The Queen's Own became the 7th Queen's Own Dragoons. Additionally in the period before the next war with the French (1756–1763) each dragoon regiment was ordered to form a Light Troop and in 1758 the Light Troops were concentrated for raids on France to distract the French from attacking Britain's ally Prussia. The raids were successful but expensive – described at the time as "breaking windows with guineas" and so they ceased. The 3rd played no further part in the war but the 7th were sent to reinforce the Allied Army fighting the French in Germany and took part in the Battles of Warburg (1760), Willinghausen (1761) and Wilhalmstel (1762) before returning home after the peace of 1763.

For the next 30 years the Regiments soldiered in Britain. In 1783 the 7th became converted to light cavalry and became the 7th (Queen's Own) Light Dragoons and as such took part in the Duke of York's campaign in the Netherlands when the British attacked the armies of revolutionary France (1794–1796). The campaign saw two battles at Beaumont and Willems in 1794 when the cavalry were very successful against the French. The 7th returned to Britain in 1795 and the four years before they next saw action were especially noteworthy, as it was in this period that Henry Paget (later Marquess of Anglesey) and Le Marchant joined. In 1789 the 7th took part in a further campaign when with Russian allies they unsuccessfully tried to force the French out of the Netherlands. In 1807 the 7th underwent a further change of title and dress when they became Hussars.

In 1808 the 7th went to join Sir John Moore's force in Spain. Having joined Moore in Galicia, they took part in the retreat to Corunna and the rearguard action at Benevente. A disaster occurred during their return to Britain as one of the troopships sank with the loss of 60 men.

The 3rd had been involved in internal security duties in England from 1802–1805 and then served in England until ordered to join Wellington in the Peninsula in 1811. They took no part in the sieges of Ciudad Rodrigo and Badajoz but as part of Le Marchant's Brigade – by now a General – they advanced into Spain. They played a major part in the Battle of Salamanca (22 July 1812) and a lesser part in Vittoria on 21 June 1813. During that year Wellington was again reinforced by the Hussar Brigade including the 7th. Neither Regiment saw further action until 1814 when the 7th Hussars fought at Orthes in France and the 3rd Dragoons at Toulouse.

Peace came in 1814 and both Regiments returned to England. However, in the summer of 1815 Napoleon escaped from Elba and the 7th were ordered to Belgium where as part of Wellington's Army they took part in the rearguard action at Genappe on 17 June and the Battle of Waterloo on 18 June. They distinguished themselves in both engagements and moved on with Wellington's Army to occupy France. Here they were joined by the 3rd Dragoons and it was in the satisfactory position of an Army of Occupation that both Regiments finished their wars with the French.

Charles Seymour, 6th Duke of Somerset   The First Colonel of the Regiment   *Attributed to Godfrey Kneller*
From a painting in the Officers' Mess

"Not every Commanding Officer has been noted on operations for his strict adherence to Dress Regulations"
Lieutenant Colonel Charles Hagart in "Mutiny" kit

Thomas Brown regaining the lost Guidon   *Attributed to Richard Ansdell*
From a painting in the Officers' Mess

Stable Duty. 3rd Hussars. Probably Aldershot. *c.* 1895

Acquiring a "Seat". 7th Hussars. Aldershot. 1930

The Passage of the Bidassoa. 7th Hussars. 13 October 1813
James Prinsep Beadle
From a painting in the Officers' Mess

"No shot was fired until they had passed the fords of the low water channel when a rocket was sent up from the steeple at Fuenterabia as a signal. Then our guns and howitzers opened fire"
From Napier's description of the battle.

The Victorian Wars

There is no generic term to describe the period in which the next campaigns took place but nearly all of them coincided in part with the reign of Victoria. When the Regiment were not abroad, they were employed in either Britain or Ireland and were often used to quell riots or maintain law. Home Service was no sinecure in the early days of the Industrial Revolution.

Before any overseas service took place, the 3rd were converted into light dragoons and became the 3rd or King's Own Light Dragoons. In 1837 the 3rd were ordered to India while in 1838 the 7th were sent to Canada to help keep the peace in the predominantly French province of Quebec. The 7th returned in 1840 but the 3rd were embarking on a tour in 1837 which would last for sixteen years and from which only 47 of the original 420 men who set out would return with the Regiment in 1853. The majority of the casualties were to be caused by disease rather than battle.

The first campaign of the 3rd was in Afghanistan where the Afghans had treacherously attacked a British force of occupation. British prisoners were held in Kabul and a British force surrounded in Jalalabad. The 3rd was part of a force sent through the Khyber Pass to relieve Jalalabad and release the prisoners. The campaign was successful and resulted in the battle honour – Cabool 1842.

In 1845–1846 the 3rd were again in action in the first Sikh War. At the time India was not a unified country in the Empire but a collection of princely states and vast areas administered by the East India Company. In December 1845, 60,000 Sikhs crossed from the Punjab into the territories of the East India Company on a quest for plunder. Within sixty days the Sikhs had been routed in a series of four major battles and the 3rd had fought with much bravery in three of these at Moodkee, Ferozeshah and Sobraon. As a result of the war the Punjab was declared a British Protectorate but the Sikhs rebelled against this in the second Sikh War in 1849. Again the Sikhs were severely defeated and the 3rd served with great distinction at the Battles of Chillianwallah and Goojerat. The 3rd took no further part in Indian Campaigns and returned to Britain in 1857. In 1861 they became an hussar regiment and were titled The 3rd King's Own Hussars.

The chance of the 7th for action in India came in 1857 when they were sent with other British forces to quell the mutiny of the native Indian troops. By the time they arrived in India much counteraction had taken place but Lucknow still required relief and the province of Oudh needed suppression. This work entailed many small actions and skirmishes when the 7th took part with columns in defeating the remnants of the mutineers. The campaign also brought the 7th two Victoria Cross awards – the first posthumously to Cornet Bankes and the second to Major Fraser. The 7th served on the NW Frontier in 1863–1864 and saw some action in 1864.

Neither Regiment saw further action until South Africa but 2 officers and 44 men of the 7th served with the Camel Corps in the Sudan in 1884 and two officers managed to get themselves attached to the 21st Lancers and charged at Omdurman.

In 1896 the 7th fought in South Africa against the revolt of the Matabele and Mashona tribesmen and in 1902 both 3rd and 7th Hussars took part in the final stage of the Boer War where they formed columns sweeping through the veldt to attack the Boers. This was to be their last action before wars came to be fought on a global scale.

The World Wars

In 1914 the 7th were part of the garrison in India while the 3rd were in England. The 3rd crossed to France in 1914 and fought there throughout the war earning 27 battle honours. Initially the 3rd fought as cavalry and even were in action with the German 3rd Hussars at one stage, but later in 1914 started to fight on foot. In 1915 they experienced gas attacks and in 1916 provided a dismounted company as part of the dismounted cavalry division. The 3rd were heavily engaged throughout the last year of the war.

The 7th were kept in Garrison Duty in India until 1917 when they were ordered to Mesopotamia to take part in the campaign against the Turks in the Euphrates and Tigris valleys. Though denied service in France as a regiment, the 7th faced much hardship in their campaign and fought as a cavalry regiment with much bravery.

In 1921 the 3rd had their final change of title when they became the 3rd The King's Own Hussars and 1922 they again saw active service as part of the Army of Occupation in Turkey. Between the wars the Regiments both served in India and at home, and in 1936 both Regiments became mechanised. The 3rd were in England when the Second World War started and the 7th in Egypt. The 3rd had some men who took part in the unsuccessful action in Norway in 1940 and then they were moved to Egypt. Both the 3rd and 7th took part in the outstanding campaign against the Italians and the reverses initially inflicted by the Germans when they joined in the desert campaign in 1941. One squadron took part in the battle for Crete and another went eastwards to Java who had the misfortune to be taken prisoner by the Japanese. In January 1942 the 7th were moved to Burma where they landed in Rangoon and then took part with great bravery in the retreat to Imphal. At the Chindwin River the 7th had to destroy their vehicles and complete the final 150 miles on foot. They reached safety in May 1942. For part of 1942 the 3rd were based in Cyprus but they returned to the desert in order to play a crucial part in the Battle of Alamein where they fought with great bravery but suffered terrible casualties.

Both the 3rd and 7th had a period of retraining and reinforcement before they saw further action. The 3rd took part in the war in Italy from April 1944 and the 7th joined the same campaign in May 1944, and it was during this campaign that the 7th formed their strong links with the Poles. The 3rd were sent to Egypt in January 1945 and then moved to the Lebanon and Syria where they remained until the war ended. The 7th continued on the advance through Italy and by the end of the war had reached Trieste.

The Post War Years

The 3rd remained in the Middle East and became the reconnaissance regiment for the 6th Airborne Division. From 1946 the 3rd were involved in internal security operations in Palestine before moving to Germany. They completed the remainder of their service prior to amalgamation in Germany. The 7th had served in Italy, Germany and England between the end of the war and 1949 and they continued to serve in Germany and England up to 1954 when they had a three year tour in Hong Kong. In 1958 the two Regiments were amalgamated at Tidworth to form The Queen's Own Hussars.

The Queen's Own Hussars have been lucky to see much of the world. They served as an armoured regiment in England and Germany from 1958 to 1967 and during that time twice had an independant squadron. "C" Squadron served in Aden from March to December 1960 and "A" Squadron in Berlin from February 1965 to February 1967. In 1967 the Regiment became an Armoured Reconnaissance Regiment equipped with armoured cars and served in Aden from July–November 1967 and in Sharjah from July 1967 to March 1968. Between 1968 and 1970 the Regiment had squadrons in Cyprus, Singapore and Hong Kong and in 1970 the Regiment came together again in Hohne as an armoured regiment. The Regiment has continued as an armoured regiment and served in both England and Germany and has completed four tours in Northern Ireland.

In the 20th Century the 7th Hussars could claim to be one of the only two surviving regiments of British regular cavalry to have been raised in Scotland.

On 31st May 1694 the future 3rd and 7th Hussars, although not yet with these titles, met for the first time when camped together by the River Meuse.

CHAPTER TWO

Battle Honours

Introduction

by Major C W M Carter
Tercentenary Coordinator

Regiments recall their history through the battle honours awarded to them. Forty of these battle honours are carried now on the Guidon.

The earliest record of the grant of a battle honour to a regiment was in 1759 when the 15th Light Dragoons were awarded "Emsdorf". However, it was not until 1844 that regulations were made standardising the recording of battle honours. Of course this involved back-dating, a process which continued for many more years; it was not until 1882 that the 3rd Hussars were awarded "Dettingen", 139 years after the battle! In addition to the 40 battle honours carried on the Guidon, the maximum for which there is room, there are a further 27 listed.

Some 5000 years ago the Egyptians attached streamers to carved wooden standards to act as rallying points for their troops in battle. Flags, as opposed to streamers, evolved in the Far East around 1000 BC. The practice spread westwards and became formalised in the standards carried in the mediaeval armies, each emblazoned with the commander's coat of arms. These standards had the additional purpose of marking the location of the commander. In the British Army they developed into the Colours of the Infantry, the Standards of the Heavy Cavalry, and the Guidons of the Light Cavalry.

The word "Guidon" is a corruption of the French "Guide Homme", the Guide Man. They became not only rallying points but also the visible symbol of the regiment's honour. As battle honours were added, so also they became memorials to all those who had fallen fighting for the regiment. They were consecrated and, when uncased, were treated with the utmost respect. It was always considered a disgrace to lose one's own Guidon and an honour to capture an enemy's.

Originally each Troop had its own Guidon, but it was not long before these were reduced to a single regimental one. However, by the 1830s the role of the light cavalry involved such dispersion that Guidons ceased to have an operational function. They were discontinued and the focal point for the regiment's loyalty became the kettledrums. Battle honours were emblazoned on the drum banners and – uniquely in the 3rd Hussars – on the uncovered silver kettledrums. Both received the same respect as a Guidon.

In 1952 King George VI reintroduced, for ceremonial purposes, the Guidons of the Light Cavalry. The first Guidon of the amalgamated Regiment was presented at Tidworth by our Colonel-in-Chief, on behalf of Her Majesty The Queen, on 20 March 1959. The Guidon is kept in the Officers' Mess and is uncased on the anniversaries of the battle honours it carries. When uncased outside the Officers' Mess it is always saluted; and carried and escorted by a Guidon Party.

On 14 May 1985 it is planned that our Colonel-in-Chief, on behalf of Her Majesty The Queen, will present the Regiment with a new Guidon. On 17 May the old Guidon will be laid up in its permanent home, Birmingham Cathedral.

In the rest of this chapter there are short articles, with eye-witness accounts where available, on the 40 battle honours.

The size of the Regimental casualty list has often been terrible and never more so than in some of those battles for which honours were granted, from El Alamein and Sidi Rezegh stretching right back to the first battle honour: Dettingen.

Three days after this battle, Brigadier General Humphrey Bland, Colonel of The King's Own Regiment of Dragoons (later the 3rd Hussars), wrote in a letter that his Regiment was "well-nigh annihilated". This was no exaggeration as the account that follows shows. Later in the year before returning to England, King George II reviewed his Army. Noticing how very weak the Regiment was he asked "sharply" whose regiment it was, and what had become of the rest. "Please, Your Majesty," the Colonel replied, "it is my regiment, and I believe that the remainder of it is at Dettingen."

Battle Honours of The Queen's Own Hussars

The following are the Battle Honours of The Queen's Own Hussars which are emblazoned on the Guidon:

DETTINGEN	3H & 7H	MARNE 1914	3H
WARBURG	7H	YPRES 1914–1915	3H
BEAUMONT	7H	CAMBRAI 1917–1918	3H
WILLEMS	7H	SOMME 1918	3H
SALAMANCA	3H	AMIENS	3H
VITTORIA	3H	FRANCE & FLANDERS 1914–1918	3H
ORTHES	7H	KHAN BAGHDADI	7H
TOULOUSE	3H	SHARQAT	7H
PENINSULA	3H & 7H	MESOPOTAMIA 1917–1918	7H
WATERLOO	7H	EGYPTIAN FRONTIER 1940	7H
CABOOL 1842	3H	BUQ BUQ	3H
MOODKEE	3H	BEDA FOMM	3H & 7H
FEROZESHAH	3H	SIDI REZEGH 1941	7H
SOBRAON	3H	EL ALAMEIN	3H
CHILLIANWALLAH	3H	NORTH AFRICA 1940–1942	3H
GOOJERAT	3H	CITTA DELLA PIEVE	3H
PUNJAUB	3H	ANCONA	7H
LUCKNOW	7H	ITALY 1944–1945	7H
SOUTH AFRICA 1901–1902	7H	CRETE	3H
RETREAT FROM MONS	3H	BURMA 1942	7H

The following Battle Honours have been awarded, but are not carried on the Guidon because the maximum allowed is forty:

SOUTH AFRICA 1902	3H	BAPAUME 1918	3H
MONS	3H	HINDENBURG LINE	3H
LE CATEAU	3H	CANAL DU NORD	3H
AISNE 1914	3H	SELLE	3H
MESSINES 1914	3H	SAMBRE	3H
ARMENTIERES 1914	3H	SIDI BARRANI	3H
GHELUVELT	3H	SIDI SULEIMAN	3H
ST JULIEN	3H	NORTH AFRICA 1940–1941	7H
BELLEWAARDE	3H	PEGU	7H
ARRAS 1917	3H	PAUNGDE	7H
SCARPE 1917	3H	CITTA DI CASTELLO	3H
ST QUENTIN	3H	RIMINI LINE	7H
LYS	3H	ITALY 1944	3H
HAZEBROUCK	3H		

Dettingen

by Major L J Melhuish
who has made a special study of this battle and has visited the battlefield

At Dettingen on 27 June 1743, the 3rd and the 7th won their first shared battle honour and captured the original silver drums. Yet that morning a French victory was probable as the Allied Army of 44,000, under King George II, withdrew along the East bank of the Main by the narrow plain under steep wooded hills, into the trap sprung by General Noilles's French Army of 70,000 from the other bank. Noilles sent 28,000 men under the Duc de Grammont over the river to bar the allies' road before Dettingen; another force crossed behind their rearguard and French batteries firing across the river commanded the lower east bank and the approaches to Dettingen. Grammont's disobedience was to forfeit the battle.

At 0800 hours the allies' advance guard located the Dettingen position and the main body came under fire from across the river. The King posted his cavalry on the left flank to cover the deployment which took until noon because the guns were at the rear of the six mile column. All this time the cavalry stood mounted under the enemy batteries. Sam Davies, an officer's servant in the 3rd, wrote "There balls was from 3 lbs to 6 lbs and 12 lbs each, our rigement was upon the left bank of the river and they playing upon us all the time".

Grammont watched the allies' confusion and, disobeying orders, left his defensive position to attack the larger allied force before it had formed. He was too late; the allies were already advancing in good order with British infantry on the left and centre and cavalry, including the 7th, on the right. The 3rd was detached to the left flank. The King marched with the first line of Infantry after his horse had bolted. In the ensuing infantry clash British musketry discipline prevailed. Grammont then launched nine squadrons of the élite Maison du Roi, in eight lines, against the allied left. The 3rd, now reduced to the strength of two weak squadrons, formed into three lines and charged the French Horse, cutting through them, causing many casualties but suffering grievously. Undaunted, they reformed and twice repeated their feat; on the last charge they cut through ten times their strength, until they had lost three-quarters of their numbers in killed and wounded.

The 7th, the Royals and later the Blues came around from the other flank and hurled themselves into the melée. The infantry, encouraged by the French cavalry's repulse, advanced and despite further French cavalry charges, Grammont's Army disintegrated, many drowning trying to cross the Main.

The 3rd's hero was Dragoon Thomas Brown who, seeing a cornet drop a standard when his wrist was wounded, "attempted to dismount in order to recover it". In so-doing he "lost two fingers of his bridle hand by a sabre cut and his horse ran away with him to the rear of the French lines". He there saw and killed a gendarme carrying off the lost standard, catching it as it fell and "fixing it between his leg and saddle" he cut his way back to the regiment, which gave him "three Huzzas". Brown received "seven wounds in his head, face and body, besides which three balls passed through his hat" and "two lodged in his back where they could not be extracted". After the battle the King, reviving the creation of Knights banneret on the field, dubbed Thomas Brown as the last.

Sam Davies had accompanied the baggage to the wood where, in 1954, the local schoolmaster said that "the ghost of a British Dragoon was sometimes seen searching for a treasure chest". Davies came under cannon fire and killed a marauding Frenchman and later took care of his badly wounded, stripped and plundered master, Major Philip Honeywood who was to recover and command the 3rd. Davies wrote "Our Rigement is above half killed and wounded, for never any Men in the Field behaved as well as they did – so carry all the Honour". Yet the Battle Honour was not awarded until 1882.

Dettingen was the last battle in which a British Monarch commanded the Army in person.

Dettingen is one of the three battle honours awarded to both the 3rd and 7th Hussars. In the case of both Regiments, it is their earliest.

The annual Regimental Day is 27th June, the anniversary of the Battle of Dettingen.

Warburg – Beaumont – Willems

by Major N G Apps
So2 on DRAC Staff

Warburg 31 July 1760

In 1756 the traditional rivalry between France and England deteriorated into the Seven Years War. The 7th Dragoons were part of the British Army deployed in support of Hannover. Twenty thousand Frenchmen under de Muy adopted a strong defence near Warburg, 25 miles southeast of Paderborn. The Marquess of Granby was ordered to attack the French right rear. The arrival two hours later of a hatless, wigless and bald Granby with 22 squadrons in the enemy's flank was decisive. Meanwhile the 7th Dragoons and the Royals did much damage on de Muy's left. Overall he lost some 8000 men and 12 guns. The British cavalry losses were small, the 7th's share being one man killed. Warburg was awarded to the Regiment in 1909. Granby's appearance resulted in the phrase "going at it baldheaded" and has been a source of inspiration for inn sign painters ever since.

Beaumont 26 April 1794

The execution of Louis XVI in 1793 brought England reluctantly into conflict with revolutionary France. Four troops of the 7th Light Dragoons had joined the allied army in the Low countries which was surprised in fog by a 30,000 strong French advance in two columns near Beaumont, 40 miles south of Brussels. Undetected, 18 allied squadrons moved to outflank the enemy's left while the 7th and 11th Light Dragoons charged the right flank, cutting through three battalions and dispersing the remainder. Over 7000 French became casualties and 41 guns and 750 prisoners were taken. The 7th's casualties were one man killed and 19 wounded. Beaumont was awarded to the 7th Hussars in 1909.

Willems 10 May 1794

The allies adopted a position between Tournai and Willems which the French attacked with the usual 30,000 men in two columns. The 7th with 14 British and two Austrian squadrons were ordered to turn the enemy's right flank as at Beaumont. The going was heavy and the French formed squares. Nine charges and artillery and infantry assistance were needed to break their formation. Some 400 prisoners and 14 guns were captured and 2000 Frenchmen became casualties. The 7th had only one man wounded and were awarded the battle honour in 1910. Not till Salamanca, 18 years later, did British cavalry again break a French square.

Salamanca – Orthes – Vittoria – Toulouse
Peninsula

by Brigadier M B Pritchard, CBE
Commanding Officer 1969–1971

The Regiment's first experiences in the Peninsula were of a disaster. A lightning invasion of Spain by Napoleon in 1808 was to drive the British Expeditionary Force to the sea at Corunna. The 7th Hussars had landed there in the Autumn. They marched inland, in reasonably good order, for about 150 miles. All were looking forward to fighting the French. Suddenly, within 10 miles of the enemy, the Army was ordered to retrace its steps. The reasons were not explained. The cavalry was to cover the retreat. It rained constantly. The dispirited Army scattered all over the countryside plundering and behaving disgracefully. The problems were not caused by the French but by the shortages of essentials like food, fodder, shoes for horses and men. All these were available but never at the right time and place. Then deep snow and biting cold added to the hideous suffering. Much reduced, the Regiment embarked for England only to lose more lives and the regimental silver off the Cornish coast.

Two years later the 3rd King's Own Dragoons landed at Lisbon to join Wellington's Army. Their first engagement in Spain was at Salamanca, about 70 miles from the Portuguese frontier. Initially there was a brief action in which the Regiment twice endured heavy French gunfire. However the French withdrew and the two armies ended up eyeing each other across the River Duoro. After two weeks of inactivity the French attacked. The Regiment fought during the withdrawal to a commanding position in the hills north of Salamanca. The opposing armies were about equal in strength but the French had reinforcements on the way. Wellington decided to stand and fight. The French advanced in an outflanking movement mistakenly thinking that the British were withdrawing. When the French were fully extended Wellington attacked. It was the early evening of a cloudless July day. The Regiment, in the foremost rank of the cavalry, charged. "Big men, on big horses, rode onward, smiting with their long glittering swords in uncontrollable power". Forty minutes later forty thousand Frenchmen were vanquished.

However an advance into Spain could not be sustained and a withdrawal to Lisbon began. It took a winter's month of dreadful hardships caused by starvation, disease and inefficiency. The rest of the winter was needed to recover before the spring advance, aimed this time at Northern Spain. After a series of outflanking movements the Battle of Vittoria was fought. Although much of the French Army escaped, it marked the liberation of Spain.

Shortly afterwards and about fifty miles away, the 7th Hussars landed on the Spanish northern coast at Bilbao. They crossed the Pyrenees and the River Bidassoa. It was Wellington's policy not to bring an action as long as the retreat continued. Nevertheless, plenty of skirmishes took place with the French cavalry. But the French stood in a strong position at Orthes behind the River Pau in southernmost France. It was a calm, bright exceptionally nice day for February. The British infantry advanced line abreast, colours flying and bands playing. The Regiment made a series of charges as the French stubbornly resisted at each position until they eventually accepted defeat. The 3rd King's Own Dragoons continued in the final advance towards Toulouse. The battle was a British victory but fought unnecessarily as unbeknownst to both contestants Napoleon had abdicated a few days earlier. Both Regiments were then to march across France to Boulogne to embark for home having earned five battle honours.

More than one hundred years before the campaigns in the Peninsula described above, the 3rd Hussars in 1702 took part in a combined operation against the Spanish port of Vigo. Their share of the prize money was £187–3s–4d.

After the Battle of Vittoria in 1813 many British regiments stole and plundered. However, not a man of the Heavy Brigade, of which the 3rd Hussars were a part, touched a heap of silver dollars which they passed on the road. General Ponsonby, the Brigade Commander, then detailed a sergeant-major to collect all the coins that his horse could carry. Later each man in the Brigade was given five of these dollars.

The 7th Hussars charging the French cavalry at Waterloo
Henry Martens
From a painting in the Officers' Mess

Trenches kit. 3rd Hussars. 1916

The taking of Rifle Wood. 3rd Hussars. 1 April 1918

The Marquess of Anglesey   *Attributed to J B Englehart*
From a painting in the Officers' Mess

Waterloo

by Lieutenant Colonel D G Pipe
currently on the Staff of S.H.A.P.E

Waterloo must be the most-documented battle in history. There are certainly excellent accounts of it in English which it would make dull reading to try to precis here. However, the engagement at Genappe is less well-known.

On 16th June 1815 the Advance Guards of the British and French Armies fought at Quatre Bras. On the 17th the British started to withdraw to the main concentration area at Waterloo. Three cavalry brigades covered this withdrawal, with Major Hodge's Squadron of the 7th Hussars acting as Rear Guard on the vital centre route. By skilful skirmishing they got back intact over the River Dyle bridge at Genappe and formed up 300 yards North of the village on the raised chaussee.

The French Lancers followed up quickly, but halted on the North edge of the village. To gain more time for the withdrawal and anticipating that a further advance by the French was imminent, Lord Uxbridge (later Lord Anglesey, Commander of the Allied Cavalry and Colonel of the 7th Hussars 1801–1842) launched the Squadron in a pre-emptive charge. In his own words "this they did most gallantly". The Lancers, wedged solidly between the houses on either side of the street and unable to retire because of the mass of cavalry pressing from behind, met the attack at the halt. Major Hodge and the French Squadron Leader were killed, but the sabres of the 7th could make no impression on the wall of lances. The Lancers then advanced, but the 7th rallied and, catching them in the open, drove them back into the village. A see-saw battle developed until Lord Uxbridge, seeing the heavy casualties suffered by the Squadron, withdrew them. He then ordered the 23rd Light Dragoons to advance, but "My address to these Light Dragoons not having been received with all the enthusiasm that I expected I ordered them to clear the chaussee". The 1st Life Guards, however, "came on with right good will" and routed the by now disorganised Lancers. The crisis of the rearguard action was over. The necessary time had been gained, but at terrible cost to the Squadron. Of some 120 men, only 19 were left in the saddle, although later in the day some of the men, all dismounted and many wounded, made their way back.

As the Regiment moved to their position on the extreme right of the Allied Line just North of Hougoumont let us take up the story in Troop Sergeant Major Cotton's words:

> 'As darkness fell on that Saturday 17 June, the Regiment joined the rest of the Army at a position about 2½ miles from Waterloo. The left squadron under Captain Verner was thrown into the valley in front of the left wing and the rest of us bivouacked near where Picton fell next day.
> The spirit of mutual defiance was such that in posting the piquets there were many little cavalry affairs.

Captain Heylinger with his troop made a spirited charge upon the enemy's cavalry and when the Duke sent to check him, his Grace desired to be made acquainted with the name of this officer who had shown so much gallantry.

Our bivouac was dismal in the extreme; what with the thunder, lightning and rain, it was as bad a night as I ever witnessed, a regular soaker. We cloaked, throwing a part over the saddle, holding by the stirrup leather to steady us if sleepy, for to lie down with water running in streams under us was not desirable and to lie amongst all the horses not altogether safe.

The dawn of that fateful day broke slowly through heavy clouds. Fortunately for most of us the excitement was too powerful to allow the physical inconvenience to be much felt. Our bivouac had a most unsightly appearance, both officers and men looked blue with cold, our long beards wet and our dirty clothing drying upon us, we were anything but comfortable.

Having been ordered to a position on the far right of the main ridge, we dismounted. Between nine and ten the Duke rode along the line and was loudly cheered as in the distance the French bands struck up. Soon the enemy's skirmishers were thrown out and they saluted our ears with that well-known music, the whistling of musket balls.

Officers and men began falling fast from the musketry of skirmishers in the standing rye and a strong line of enemy cavalry passed Hougemont to their left and ascended to our position regardless of our artillery fire. 7H led against them and after a few cuts and points the enemy went about.

The French guns continued with great vigour and was the most furious cannonade I ever witnessed. Under it came Ney's cavalry, which was a stupendous force compared with ours and the menacing approach of the French who rode amongst and around our squares was not quietly witnessed by our own horsemen. My horse was killed by roundshot, but I was soon mounted again on a cuirassier's. As onset followed onset in rapid succession we made many spirited charges between the British squares, but before one assault was met and repulsed another was prepared and pressing on.

When our gallant infantry finally broke the Emperor's Old Guard, we followed them until we came up with the Prussians and as they passed us (for I had the honour and good fortune to be an actor on this scene,) I heard their bands play "God Save the King!", which soul-stirring compliment we returned with hearty cheers.'

No Regimental account can close without paying tribute to the courage and stoicism of the Colonel of the Regiment, on both days always well forward as each crisis developed. Near the end of the battle, riding next to the Duke of Wellington, he was hit by grapeshot. His leg had to be amputated. His A.D.C. commented 'He never moved or complained ... He said once, perfectly calmly, that he thought that the instrument was not very sharp'.

Every year on June 18th, circumstances permitting, the Regiment celebrates the victory at Waterloo as a holiday.

Cabool 1842 – Moodkee – Ferozeshah – Sobraon – Chillianwallah – Goojerat – Punjaub

by Major R C McDuell
Served 1949–1968

The operations in Afghanistan in 1842 and the two campaigns of 1845–1848 and 1849–1852 against the Sikhs were but three of almost 70 "small wars" in which the British Army was involved between Waterloo and the Crimea. They were, however, three of the hardest if not the hardest in which the British Army was involved in the Indian Sub-Continent.

The British in India had for many years viewed with concern the traditional incursions by Imperial Russia into Afghanistan and, when in 1838, negotiations with the Afghan ruler failed, an expedition was sent across the North West Frontier and a puppet placed on the throne. Over the next two years the situation deteriorated and in November 1841 revolution broke out with the assassination of three senior British Officials. Two months later the Garrison in Kabul began its tragic withdrawal with only the Doctor of the Essex Regiment reaching Jalalabad alive to tell the tale.

Immediately steps were taken to rescue those people still trapped in Kabul, and to punish the Afghans for their treachery. The 3rd Light Dragoons, with close on 600 officers and men, were, in January 1842, despatched to Ferozepore. They arrived on 18 February but were immediately ordered to Peshawar. As was the practise in those days the senior commanding officer, in this case White, of the 3rd, was appointed to command the Brigade, and the Regiment was led, with great distinction throughout the campaign, by Major George Lockwood. In late February the force set out across the Punjab for Afghanistan. The journey is best described by Walter Unett at the time:

> 'We crossed the Stulej on the 22nd ultimo, by a bridge of boats, and were obliged to pass over in single file, which took 2 whole days ... We were detained seven days crossing the Ravi. ... This is a great misfortune, as we were ordered to do the 31 marches to Peshawar in 21 days. You can have no idea of crossing a river in boats. We have camels with us and many have actually to be lifted into the boats. They are the most obstinate devils alive ...
>
> Peshawar is the hottest place in India, so I hope that we may not remain long there, but push on and force the Khyber Pass and relieve General Sale at Jalalabad. ... I hope that the King's Own Dragoons may gain such a name as will never be forgotten – in India, at least.'

Reaching Peshawar on 29 March the force lost no time in entering the Khyber Pass, reaching Jalalabad on 16 April where they were welcomed by the beleaguered garrison and the Band of the 13th Light Infantry playing "You are very late in coming".

The Regiment was to spend the next four months in Jalalabad plagued by flies and exploited by the contractors before the decision was taken to withdraw the whole force to Kabul. It was in fact a fighting withdrawal, with the force, of which the Regiment were part, having to face the bulk of Akbar Khan's army which was 20,000 strong. The Regiment was involved in various running battles before it reached Kabul on 15 September, and one of these is again well described by Unett in one of his numerous letters:

> 'My squadron was ordered to support the Irregular Horse. So away we went, drew swords, and formed on their right. In our front was the bed of a river, about 15 or 20 yards broad with steep banks. Fisher and Bowles were my troop leaders. On the opposite bank were two of the enemy's Horse, with numbers in rear of them. When close to the bank, one of the men on the opposite side presented his matchlock to me. I could see along the barrel. It flashed in the pan. I turned to Fisher and said, 'Misfired, by Jove!' I never took my eyes off the rascal. I pushed my horse over the bank, charged across, and the only thing I did not recollect is how I got up the opposite bank, as my grey Arab cannot jump at all. On seeing me charge, the enemy went about, and had got about 20 yards start on me. In an instant, however, I was beside the fellow, and at the pace I was going – about 20 miles an hour – without the slightest exertion passed my sword through his body.
>
> I then made a thrust at his friend. The place where I overtook them was a steep slippery bank with a ditch full of water; and when pressing my sword to thrust at the fellow, his hind legs sunk in the ditch and he fell backwards upon me. The dead man lay upon my right and his horse in the ditch. The other man and his horse were scrambling up the bank, with his sword flashing in my face. I could touch his horse, and had he tumbled back he would have fallen on the point of my sword. He was killed within a few yards. I saw him rolling on the ground, while one of my men was cutting at him.
>
> Having had much the start of my squadron, I was now in danger of being ridden over by my own men, as they were rushing on; but my horse was active and strong and with little to carry, and after a few struggles he got up on to his legs again. I never lost the reins, and was on his back again in an instant, and in about 200 yards regained my place again in the front and found my men cutting up the enemy in small parties. . . .
>
> All the officers and men of our regiment distinguished themselves. Fisher and Bowles killed several men with their own hands, and Yerbury had a narrow escape of being killed. His clothes were cut and his horse received a deep sabre wound in the neck. We captured a few of their horses. One of our men sold one . . . to our Colonel for £30. My Sgt. Major caught one and I could have taken another, but I had something else to do just then'.

To all intents and purposes the second Afghan war ended on 15 September 1842 and exactly two years later the Regiment learned that Her Majesty had been greatly pleased to permit it to bear the distinction "Cabool 1842" in commemoration of past services in the second campaign in Afghan. At the same time all ranks who had served in the campaign were awarded the medal with the inscription "Cabool 1842". This was the first occasion that the 3rd had been so rewarded, since although many of their predecessors had fought in the campaigns in the Peninsula, the Military General Service Medal was not granted until 1845 and issued to those recipients who were still alive and could be traced in 1857.

It was to be another three years before the 3rd Light Dragoons would again see action, but whilst this was a period of comparative peace and quiet it was one during which they suffered severely from death and illness. Their next adversaries were to be the Sikhs whose ruler, Ranjit Singh, the Lion of the Punjab, had for many years been seeking ways of annexing parts of British

India. To this end he had created a highly trained army organised on French lines and employing many French emigre officers which, by the time that Ranjit Singh died in 1839, had established itself in a strong position within the Sikh nation.

Following the death of Ranjit Singh in 1839 there were many within the Sikh Army who urged the Government in Lahore to invade British India. These factions were encouraged by the initial success of the rebels in Afghanistan and by the end of 1845 had, in effect, despite the opposition of the Lahore Government, decided to invade. That the intentions of the Sikh army, the Khalsa, had been known to the authorities in India is not in doubt. What, therefore, comes as a surprise is the comparative lack of preparedness of the British troops and those of the East India Company, and whilst the Governor General had in fact gone to Ludhiana very few of the regiments that were to form the Army of the Sutlej were on any sort of alert, and none of them had moved when the Sikhs crossed the Sutlej.

The 3rd were ordered to start the 120 mile march from Ambala on the 11 December to be followed by the infantry on the 12th, and after a long and tiring march the army had reached the area of Moodkee by the early hours of the 18 December. This was to be a significant day in the long and distinguished history of the Regiment when it was to lose 61 officers and men killed and 35 wounded, and when the charge, for which it later became famous, was to be described in a despatch written on the following day by the Commander-in-Chief in the following words:

> '... With praiseworthy gallantry, the Third Light Dragoons, and the second brigade of cavalry ... turned the left of the Sikh army, and sweeping along the whole rear of its infantry and guns, silenced for a time the latter, and put their numerous cavalry to flight'.

It was as a result of their actions at Moodkee that they were to receive the sobriquet "Shaitan-Ke-Bachche" – "The Devil's Children" from their Sikh adversaries.

In spite of their considerable efforts and losses on the 18th the 3rd, with the rest of Gough's army, were kept under arms throughout the night expecting another attack from the Sikh army. Both the Cavalry Brigades were commanded by officers of the 3rd Light Dragoons and the Regiment was in turn under the command of Major C W M Balders who led it with great gallantry until severely wounded in the action of the 19 December, and for which he was to be promoted a Brevet Colonel and created a Companion of the Bath.

On the 20th the Regiment was directed to Ferozeshah and after a journey of some seven hours was deployed early on that morning some two miles from the Sikh entrenchments. The battle began at 3.30 in the afternoon, but after the infantry had suffered severe casualties the 3rd, comprising 416 officers and men, were directed to attack the eastern face of the Sikh position. This glorious occasion is best described in the words of Fortescue who wrote:

> 'the 3rd charged headlong over the entrenchments, cut down the Sikh gunners, and then swept with loud shouts over tent-pegs, tent-ropes, guns and every description of obstance, straight through the Sikh

reserves to the opposite side of the enemy's position, where they rallied, having lost half their number, a mere handful of unconquerable men'.

Once again the 3rd suffered severe casualties with 55 killed and 93 wounded, and whilst they were to take part in the third major action at Sobraon the words again of Sir John Fortescue described very clearly what the Regiment achieved at Ferozeshah:

'The heroes of the action were beyond doubt the Third Light Dragoons. It is rare for cavalry to charge entrenched artillery; and only troopers of rare devotion and discipline would have faced such a trial. The Third had lost nearly one hundred men and over one hundred and twenty horses on the 18th December; they lost one hundred and fifty-two more men and sixty horses on the 21st; yet the remnant without hesitation charged and defeated superior numbers of Sikh cavalry on the 22nd. Few regiments of horse in the world can show a finer record of hardihood and endurance.'

Shortly before the final major action of the campaign, the Battle of Sobraon, in which they also took part, the Commander-in-Chief, Sir Henry Hardinge, paid the Regiment the rare compliment of addressing its Commanding Officer in front of the whole army with the words:

'Colonel White, your regiment is an honour to the British Army, and I wish you to make known these my sentiments, as head of this government, to your officers and men.'

Once again a charge by the Regiment was to play a significant part at Sobraon; but on this occasion the casualties were light, amounting to 5 killed and 27 wounded. This saw the end of the first Sikh war, but it is interesting to note that a small party of recruits on its way to join the Regiment had in fact fought with the 16th Lancers at the Battle of Aliwal. On 13 February the Regiment crossed the Sutlej with Gough's army and rode to Lahore where a British resident was appointed to direct a Regency Council governing the Protectorate of the Punjab.

In the two years immediately following the signing of the peace at Lahore the 3rd remained at Ambala. Early in 1848 came news of the revolt at Multan in which two British officials had been murdered. Although of itself a matter of no great consequence, the situation was allowed to deteriorate and, in spite of efforts by the Governor-General to uphold the authority of the Sikh government, a continual stream of Sikh troops defected and the reluctant decision was taken that the rebels must be put down.

Accordingly, on the 20 October the 3rd Light Dragoons, as part of the Army of the Punjab, crossed the Sutlej and advanced northward. Although there were two actions in November of that year the 3rd played only a small part and their casualties were small. 13 January 1849 found the British Army advancing on the Sikh rebels in the area of Chillianwallah, and it was at about 3 o'clock on that afternoon that the 3rd made its now famous charge against the rebel Sikh cavalry. The Regiment's losses were 24 killed and 24 wounded and the Commander-in-Chief described the battle in his despatch as follows:

> 'Sir Joseph Thackwell names with much satisfaction Brigadier White's conduct of his brigade, Major Yerbury commanding Third Light Dragoons, and the gallant charge of Captain Unett in command of a squadron of that corps. And the Right Honourable the Governor-General of India, Major-General Sir Joseph Thackwell, K.C.B., K.H., for his services; and to Brigadier White for his conduct of the brigade of cavalry on the left.'

As in previous campaigns the Regiment was commanded by its Senior Major, in this case Yerbury, whilst Colonel White was appointed to command the 1st Cavalry Brigade in the rank of Brigadier.

Three days later came the surrender of the fortress at Multan. On 7 February Lieutenant-Colonel Lockwood rejoined the Regiment from England and was immediately appointed to command the 2nd Cavalry Brigade, also in the rank of Brigadier. The final battle of the second Sikh war was fought at Goojerat on 21 February 1849 when a British force numbering about 27,000 faced a Sikh rebel army in excess of 60,000. Walter Unett who had been badly wounded at Chillianwallah had by now recovered and returned to command his squadron of the 3rd for this most decisive battle. The Regiment's casualties on this occasion were described in the regimental history as "very trifling", and to quote Unett:

> '... great was the slaughter. My squadron was attached to Captain Blood's troops of the Horse Artillery ... At close quarters, in trees, bushes, hollows, villages, cornfields etc. – at the lowest calculation every other shot told, so that my poor squadron is fully repaid for our loss at Chillianwallah ...'

The 3rd had fought with great distinction in the Sikh Wars suffering numerous casualties and being granted no less than five battle honours. Their senior officers had commanded cavalry brigades with great distinction and the 3rd Light Dragoons had created for itself a unique niche in the history of British India.

From 1838 to 1842 – while the 3rd Hussars were in India – the 7th Hussars served in Canada, sent there with the KDGs because of a minor rebellion in the area of Montreal.

Lucknow

by Lieutenant M J Shattock
Troop Leader "A" Squadron

In response to the Indian Mutiny the 7th Hussars were duly despatched, arriving in Allahabad in November 1857. After Delhi's recapture, Oudh remained under revolt, the town of Lucknow being integral to the retention of British supremacy in the region.

Despite putting up brave resistance, the grossly outnumbered garrison force had been evacuated in September 1857. A combined force, with the 7th Hussars at its forefront, under the British Commander-in-Chief Sir Colin Campbell, then set about retaking the town in March 1858. Some 21 days of fierce fighting ensued, the British forces being vastly outnumbered. The 7th carried out charge after charge with "the bravery, relentlessness and rapidity, characteristic of a fine Cavalry Regiment". Eventually Lucknow was recaptured and Oudh was saved.

The 7th continued its gallant work, mopping up the remnants of the mutineers. In one such operation at Masa Bagh on 19 March 1858, the Regiment won its first Victoria Cross, awarded to Cornet William Bankes. He was escorting two horse artillery guns. The citation continues the story:

> 'They unlimbered and fired a couple of shells, when, to everybody's astonishment, about fifty villagers, maddened with bhang or opium, and led by the daroga, or headman – an enormously tall fellow – rushed out straight upon the guns. Hagart (the Seventh's Commanding Officer) ordered the Seventh to charge, and one of the first men down was Captain Slade of "H" Troop. With the greatest gallantry, Cornet Bankes led on the troop, and shot three of the rebels at the same moment that Lieutenant Wilkin had his foot nearly cut through. Wilkin's horse, a stallion, would not leave the ranks, and everything devolved on the young cornet. Unhappily his bravery was unavailing. A young mutineer, a mere boy, dropped to his knee and hamstrung Bankes' horse with a slash of his tulwar, and, the Cornet's revolver being empty, he went down at the mercy of the fiends, who did not know what mercy meant.'

However, Colonel Hagart soon galloped in with reinforcements to quell the melée, and was himself only denied a VC because his rank was considered "too high". Bankes died from his wounds some three days later and was awarded the Victoria Cross posthumously.

It is the bold Colonel Hagart whose photograph appears between pages 12 and 13 whose attire seems to epitomise the fact that standardisation of dress and deportment has long been a problem in the Regiment.

Hagart's successor, Lieutenant-Colonel Russell, led the Regiment in December 1858 in the Trans-Gogra Campaign crossing various rivers in pursuit of the infamous Nana Sahib's band of rebels. They met on the River Raptee on 31 December, and during the ensuring debacle the Regiment won its second Victoria Cross. The river became a scene of ugly fighting and confusion, horses and riders being swept off their feet by the strong current. In this context, Major Charles Fraser displayed, according to the citation:

> '... conspicuous and cool gallantry in having volunteered, at great personal risk, and under a sharp fire of musketry, to swim to the rescue of Captain Stisted and some men of the Seventh Hussars, who were in imminent danger of being drowned in the River Raptee, while in pursuit of the rebels. Major Fraser succeeded in this gallant service, although at the same time partially disabled, not having recovered from a severe wound received while leading a squadron in a charge against some fanatics in the action of Nawab-Gange on the 13th June, 1858.'

Following this action, Brigadier Horsford, CB, commanding the Field Force commented:

> 'For over a year the Seventh Hussars have been attached to this force, and during that time their behaviour has been such as to secure them universal esteem ... the just pride which has guided all ranks not only in the face of the enemy, but also in camp, will ever cause them to retain the reputation they have so well earned.'

On 3 September 1863 Queen Victoria awarded "Lucknow" as a battle honour in recognition of the Regiment's success during the Indian Mutiny.

Cornet Bankes, VC, was the only British soldier killed in the Indian Mutiny whose body was buried in a coffin.

The 7th Hussars spent the hot summer of 1858 rounding up mutineers. The Regiment had sixty-seven casualties at the Battle of Nawabganj; but in the following few weeks thirty-three died from "sunstroke". Many "fell asleep in their tents and never awoke". 250 more had to be evacuated to hospital.

South Africa 1901–1902

by Major T J Thomas
Second-in-Command 1970–1972

At the outbreak of the Boer War in 1899, 240 reservists rejoined the 7th Hussars at Norwich, but 395 horses had to be sent to South Africa. Continual drafts were also despatched, including one of 120 to the 14th Hussars. Fourteen officers went out, earning three DSOs.

However, it was not until late November 1901 that the 7th Hussars sailed from Southampton, under command of Lieutenant-Colonel The Honourable R T Lawley, landing at Capetown. Sixteen horses died on passage. On New Years Eve 1901 disaster struck at De Aar, after a 350 mile rail journey. The veterinary surgeon shot a horse in the lines and the remainder bolted, flattening tents and bursting through the perimeter wire. Despite a trumpeter sounding "Feed" it was a week before strays were rounded up from the veldt.

The Boers by now were strategically defeated. Their farms were razed and families put in concentration camps. But strong well mounted commandos roamed the veldt, armed with Mauser rifles, Maxim machine guns and field artillery. To counter them, cavalry and mounted infantry columns were based at rail heads, with artillery support, carrying out drives against block house lines or other columns, in the effort to trap the commandos. In this setting the 7th Hussars joined the Bays at Windburgh, to form a column under Colonel Lawley.

Local clearing operations began in appalling wet weather. The diary for 16 February 1902 read: "Up to date the total bag was 7 Boers, some cattle and horses".

On 31 March 1902 the column defeated General Pretorious' Commando at Boschmans Kop, largely thanks to Major John Vaughan, the 7th Hussars Intelligence Officer and later to be Inspector of Cavalry of BEF 1914. He had spent six nights observing the veldt, with a Boer guide and Kaffir tracker, when he saw 25 Boers move into a derelict farm. By 0100 he had led the Bays forward and scattered the Boer horse lines. Hearing the rattle of a cart he galloped off alone and captured General Pretorious. The Bays dug in, and Major Vaughan was wounded in the knee at dawn, losing his first horse when checking the pickets. As he started to lead a withdrawal, Major Vaughan lost his second horse. Seeing 150 mounted Boers outflanking the position, he gave the order to charge, to find: "A fatal mistake; in the craze for mounted rifles the Bays had handed in their swords." Help was at hand: "A blessed sight. I saw the advanced guard of the 7th Hussars cantering over the open veldt." They drew swords to charge and the Boers fled. As he galloped back to Colonel Lawley, Major Vaughan's third horse was shot under him. For this courage he was awarded the DSO.

The war ended in 1902.

France 1914–1918

by Lieutenant-Colonel D J M Jenkins
Commanding Officer

The 3rd Hussars fought throughout the whole of the Great War in France. They mobilised in August 1914 and departed from England and did not return home until the Autumn of 1919. During the war they gained 27 battle honours but lost 13 officers and 94 other ranks killed and 27 officers and 358 other ranks wounded. While these figures are low compared with the total losses in the war, it should be noted that the maximum strength of the Regiment at any one time was 28 officers and 591 other ranks. Thus over 100% of the officer establishment and 77% of the other ranks establishment became a casualty and drafts of conscripts were used to keep the Regiment up to strength.

The actual fighting can be split into three phases – firstly in the opening weeks of the war when there was considerable movement. This was followed by over three years of trench warfare battles when the strategic aim was to force "a gap" in the enemy lines of trenches so that the cavalry could deploy through this for their traditional role. Finally the last period of the war in 1918 again saw considerable movement in the fighting. Throughout the war in France the fighting was on such a scale and involved such large numbers that the Regiment was only in a position of contributing to the whole and – in common with all regiments – was not offered the chance of an individual action that would make a change to the whole campaign. Thus the history of the Regiment in France is dictated by the moves of the allies (the British and French) and the Germans.

The 3rd Hussars reached France on 14 August and with the 1st Cavalry Division crossed into Belgium and advanced towards Mons on 21 August. Contact was made with the Germans on 22 August when the outnumbered British met the advancing Germans. There followed 13 days of mobile war as the allies were forced back in the retreat from Mons towards Paris. The Regiment was involved in the battle at Le Cateau when the British tried to hold the advance and throughout the period fought many skirmishes with the German cavalry and infantry – they even fought the 3rd German Hussars in one such skirmish. The Germans were finally held just east of Paris and then the allies counter attacked over the Marne. The Regiment was involved in this battle and then in the race north as each side tried to outflank the other. This involved bitter fighting both on horse and on foot and finally dismounted action in embryo trenches when the Germans tried to penetrate the British lines. The line of trenches adopted became the basis of the war for the next three years. By November the 3rd Hussars had fought in both a withdrawal and an advance, as cavalry and as infantry, and had won eight battle honours.

Once the trench lines were established, the tendency was to hold the cavalry back and to try to force "a gap". However the lines of trenches became so complex and the defensive fire of machine guns and artillery so lethal that the gaps never came. In 1915 there were periods when the Regiment was held in billets in the rear when they managed to play polo and have normal cavalry training. This was interspersed with periods in the trenches and they were used in emergencies to hold the line as infantry. One such case in 1915 was at the second battle of Ypres when the Germans caused considerable confusion by the first use of gas. The RSM at the time – RSM Smith – was given a DCM for his gallantry and resourcefulness in steadying the gas-filled infantry.

By 1916 the British could no longer afford the manpower luxury of having the cavalry uncommitted to the daily warfare and casualties of the trenches and so the 3rd Hussars formed an Infantry Company of 8 officers and 300 men to serve in the trenches and later a Machine Gun Squadron. The 3rd were ready at the Somme in 1916 to exploit "the Gap" but were not committed to the battle. They waited for a similar opportunity at Vimy Ridge in 1917 but again the chance did not come. In between these major battles the Regiment served tours in the trenches and suffered small numbers of casualties. It was as infantry that they took part in the bitter fighting of the Battle of Cambrai in 1917. This saw the first major successful use of tanks by the British and in the considerable gain made by the allies there was some confusion of where the front line was. This was exploited by the two Officers' Mess staff of "B" Squadron who bicycled forward to join their Squadron. They reached Cambrai and found a food store where they helped themselves to what they wanted. It then occurred to them that this was a German store and "the awful truth of their situation" was apparent. They bicycled back to the British without interference from the Germans and gave their officers a "'scrumptious dinner" on captured food.

In 1918 the whole pattern of the fighting changed. The collapse of the Russians in 1917 allowed the Germans to redeploy their Eastern Front Force to the west. In March 1918 the Germans attacked and for 12 days advanced to Amiens. The 3rd Hussars were involved in bitter fighting on foot especially at Rifle Wood which prevented the enemy taking Amiens. Eight immediate awards for gallantry were given to the Regiment for their fighting that day. The German advance was held and the allies were joined by American Forces. This enabled them to counter attack and the Regiment fought with the cavalry as the allies advanced north-east. In the process they gained a further seven battle honours and during the war earned a total of 93 awards. These and the honours – both those carried on the Guidon and the others such as Aisne, Arras and Bapaume – testify to the continued spirit and bravery displayed by the 3rd Hussars.

3rd King's Own (Light) Dragoons. 1835 *J Matthews* From a painting in the possession of Major R C Bagnell (Served in the Regiment 1954–1977)

Victory at Beda Fomm. 3rd Hussars. February 1941

Khan Baghdadi – Sharqat – Mesopotamia 1917–1918

by Captain S Jackson
Training Adjutant

"My aim, gentlemen, is the complete destruction of all Turkish Forces downstream of Ava." With these words, at 1000 hrs on 25 March 1918, the 7th Hussars entered the First World War after 3½ years of boredom and frustration in India. Four months earlier the Regiment had arrived in Mesopotamia (now Iraq) to join the 11th Cavalry Brigade. By 19 March they had marched 500 miles to Baghdad and completed intensive training (which included an officer finishing third in the Baghdad Grand National!). The Brigade task was "to move with rapidity and boldness and to act vigorously against the Turkish right flank or rear" – a cavalryman's dream.

Despite the loss, due to illness, of the Commanding Officer, the Regiment set off up the Euphrates, and managed to outflank the enemy, cutting off the Turkish line of retreat. "B" and "C" Squadrons routed the withdrawing Turks by machine-gun and rifle fire forcing the Turks to attempt to bypass the position. The Turks then marched into "A" and "D" Squadrons. This action resulted in the Turkish 50th Division ceasing to be a viable operational formation. The Regiment concluded its task by leading the Brigade into Ava on 28 March.

The Regiment were then moved into a summer camp about 50 miles west of Baghdad in a desolate tract of desert. Kitchens were erected, tables and chairs constructed and the desert irrigated to produce grass for the horses. Fish were caught using grenades!

Until October the Regiment was involved in the tedious routine of training, exercising and feeding horses, cleaning tack and preparing for inspections. Problems were aggravated by dysentery, malaria and even influenza. However, on 4 October the Regiment was again ordered to operations.

In an effort to force Turkey's withdrawal from the war, the Army was tasked to seize as much ground as possible up the Tigris River. The Regiment was to turn the left flank of the enemy positioned at the Fat-ha gorge and to block their line of retreat.

The initial daylight attempt to cross a tributary north of Fat-ha failed; however, during darkness the Regiment shot-up a supply column and, for some inexplicable reason, all the enemy withdrew. The Brigade, less "B" Squadron who guarded the baggage, crossed the Tigris on 27 March. During the next few days the Regiment was in contact at squadron level. Heavy fighting resulted in 70 casualties with a large loss of officers and NCOs.

On 30 October the enemy surrendered and on 1 November Turkey signed an Armistice; the Mesopotamian campaign was over. During the course of operations the Regiment lost 224 all ranks, killed, wounded, sick or missing.

Egyptian Frontier 1940 – Sidi Barrani – Buq Buq – Beda Fomm – Sidi Suleiman – North Africa 1940–1942

The 7th Hussars, mechanised early in 1937, used the time from then until the entry of Italy into the war in June 1940 to good purpose: training in the desert. In spite of a pedestrian advance along the coast by the much more numerous Italian Army, the desert inland was dominated by the small British force in a series of actions in which the regiment earned the battle honour "Egyptian Frontier 1940". The Italians stopped, dug in, but were ejected in the battles around 'Sidi Barrani.'

Meanwhile, the 3rd Hussars, who had been stationed in England in the early months of the war, did not arrive in Egypt until the end of September 1940. However, by November they were in action. Although at Sidi Barrani their Brigade was in reserve, in the subsequent operations the 3rd Hussars were awarded the battle honour "Buq Buq". In the subsequent pursuit of the Italians, now retreating along the coast, an outflanking group, which included both the 3rd and 7th Hussars, moved across the desert to cut them off. In an engagement at Mechili, Trooper John Bell was awarded the MM:

> 'Trooper Bell was the gunner in a Cruiser Tank. During the action two out of three Cruisers were put out of action. On the order to withdraw, the tank which Trooper Bell was in could not be made to start for ten minutes, during which at least 8 enemy Medium Tanks had approached to within 400 yards.
> 'Trooper Bell, single-handed kept up an extremely rapid (55 rounds in ten minutes), determined and accurate fire and accounted for at least two of the enemy tanks, and certainly kept the remainder at bay. It was the cool action on the part of this gunner that enabled the two damaged tanks to limp out of action, and undoubtedly saved the crew of his own tank.'

Two days earlier near Tobruk, Sergeant Patrick Cleere (now Major P Cleere, MBE, DCM, Quartermaster 1962–1970) was awarded the DCM for twice dismounting under heavy fire to attach tow-ropes to his troop leader's mined tank and then, after both tanks had been hit, rescuing the survivors.

At "Beda Fomm", the first shared battle honour since "Peninsula" 127 years earlier, the Italian Army was trapped and destroyed completely.

By April 1941, when the Germans attacked, the British had had to withdraw many of their regiments, including the 7th Hussars, to refit to fight in Greece and elsewhere. After the retreat, squadrons of the 3rd Hussars were in action in the defence of Tobruk and in Crete. In June a composite squadron earned the further battle honour of "Sidi Suleiman" before the whole Regiment came together again in Cyprus.

Crete 1941

by Major Roy Farran, DSO, MC

A squadron of light tanks had been hastily put together under Major Gilbert Peck in May 1941. The Germans had driven allied forces off the Greek mainland, but a mixed force had held on to Crete. Not surprisingly, there was a shortage of heavy weapons, artillery and ammunition. Dive-bombers sank the ship carrying our tanks in Suda Bay. By some miracle, with Hussars working as stevedores, we got them ashore in lighters.

Two troops were detached to the airfields at Heraklion and Rhetimo, farther east. These troops successfully defended those two airstrips which were never taken by the enemy until we retreated.

We, in the west, were not so lucky. At breakfast on 20 May, the sky was filled by German aircraft, strafing very low. Then the parachutists came. Thousands of them. Many were killed on the way down or soon after landing, but our own casualties were just as heavy.

I and one tank went off in the confusion to the key village of Galatas. Then I was sent to support hard-pressed New Zealanders in the same area. We took small parties of paratroopers by surprise in the cemetery, around our own field hospital which they had occupied, near a Greek prison at Agya, and in Galatas itself.

After a few days we were ordered west to support a counter-attack on Malame airfield. Sergeant Skedgewell was in the lead tank and ran into a captured anti-aircraft gun. He was mortally wounded, but Cook, his wounded driver, brought the tank back.

Our communications were so bad that Headquarters thought we had failed when in reality we had reached the edge of the airfield. A withdrawal was ordered.

When the enemy tried to outflank us, through Galatas, we supported the New Zealanders in a bayonet charge. On our first pass through the village, one tank was hit but was still operational. Two New Zealand infantrymen replaced our wounded hussars. Then, on the second attack, my tank was knocked out and we were all wounded. If you ever visit Crete, you will find that a piece from a 3rd Hussar tank is a garden gate near the centre of Galatas. The rest of the Squadron covered the allied retreat to the beaches at Sphakia on the south side.

The historians say we caused such casualties to the German airborne that they could never again mount a full-scale parachute attack.

Sidi Rezegh

by Lieutenant-Colonel J Congreve, DSO, OBE
Then "C" Squadron Leader

In November 1941 at Sidi Rezegh the 7th Hussars, as the 3rd Hussars a year later at El Alamein, were to fight their most desperate battle of the war. In it their most loved CO, Colonel Freddie Byass, was killed and there were a great many casualties and missing.

The army plan by General Cunningham was to seize vital ground at ridge from Sidi Rezegh south-east with three armoured brigades to bring the enemy armour to battle and destroy it, and at the same time to attack and help the Tobruk garrison break out.

This plan was going well and on 20 November the situation was that 7th Armoured Division with 7th Armoured Brigade and support group were on Sidi Rezegh. The 4th and 22nd Armoured Brigades were deployed south-east, both having had engagements with the enemy armour.

The plan for 21 November was for 7th Armoured Brigade to do a limited attack to secure the crest of escarpment overlooking the vital road "Trig Capuzzo" while 30 Corps continued to advance up the coast to Tobruk.

At first light on the 21st the 11th Hussars reported large numbers of tanks and infantry moving towards Sidi Rezegh. The 7th Hussars halted and turned round with orders to move south-east to delay the enemy. The 7th Hussars advanced south-east with "A" Squadron right and "B" Squadron left and RHQ "C" Squadron in reserve. As it grew lighter "A" Squadron came under fire from 2000 yards from anti-tank guns used boldly between the tanks and at the same time "B" Squadron was also heavily engaged. It appeared that 100 plus tanks were attacking the Regiment. "C" Squadron was ordered on to the left of "B" Squadron and soon were heavily engaged; so was RHQ. At this time the CO ordered "C" Squadron to move to the left to help "A" Squadron who were being overrun. OC "C" Squadron was giving this order when his microphone was shot out of his hand and the wireless mast shot away. Not all of "C" Squadron, therefore, moved over.

The fighting was very heavy and most tanks saw their shots bouncing off the enemy tanks but did cause casualties on anti-tank guns. OC "C" Squadron had to move to three tanks to keep control as each was knocked out. Eventually Marcus Fox picked him up and command was continued.

The Regiment at this time was ordered to withdraw slowly to RHQ and the enemy seemed to have moved north though there were pockets everywhere. All moving tanks were collected and retired on RHQ who tried to rejoin the Brigade but found the enemy between and so were ordered south-east to contact 4th Armoured Brigade. Major Fosdick managed to move between enemy columns and the Regiment eventually halted about 15 miles south-east and contacted a 4th Hussar Troop who asked for medical help and supplies.

The Regiment then leagured, with six tanks all carrying wounded and men picked up, short of petrol and ammunition.

It had been an expensive battle for the Brigade. The 7th Hussars had lost its CO, Major Younger of "B" Squadron, wounded with a great many others, "A" Squadron overrun and taken prisoner and "C" Squadron still with four tanks and two to join with Tim Llewellyn-Palmer next day – a total for the Regiment of eight tanks. But the enemy were denied the vital ground and the attack north was successful.

The tanks of 7th Armoured Brigade, armed with 2 pdrs, were massively outgunned by the German 75 mm on their Pz Mk IV and the even more lethal high-velocity 50 mm on their Pz Mk III. The latter could knock out our tanks from about 1500 yards while our 2 pdr rounds bounced off their frontal armour even at close range.

By 1941 the 7th Hussars had been in existence for 252 years. During this time they had often fought alongside the Germans, but until then never against them. The Desert was the first occasion. In the First World War of course the 7th Hussars were fighting the Turks.

Pegu – Paungde – Burma 1942

by Colonel J F Astley-Rushton
then Headquarters Squadron Leader, 7th Hussars

In January 1942 the 7th Armoured Brigade, of which the 7th Hussars were a part, embarked to reinforce Malaya. However, when the fall of Singapore became imminent, the Brigade was diverted at sea to the defence of Burma. Arriving just before Rangoon was captured, the Regiment found the docks virtually deserted and manned the cranes themselves to complete the unloading of all the tanks, vehicles and ammunition within 24 hours. The 7th Hussars had now that most difficult of operations: a withdrawal amidst paddy and jungle against a ruthless and experienced enemy.

Much of the fighting involved clearing road blocks established by the Japanese who had by-passed the withdrawing army. From one of these actions comes one of the most remarkable stories of the war:

Lieutenant Patteson, the lead tank, negotiated at night and under fire a difficult road block. Reporting that he was through, he drove on, but soon after his tank was hit, plunged down an embankment, and ended upside down. In the darkness and confusion Patteson became separated from his crew. He stumbled into a Japanese position, was captured and brutally interrogated. Having revealed nothing, the Japanese tied him to the road block, knowing full well that the Brigade had to break through here; and that to do so they would have to fire on, and subsequently ram, the road block. After two hours the 25 pdrs, unaware of his predicament, opened fire. Without even touching him, a shell fragment loosened one of his bonds. At that moment some cattle stampeded and Patteson, his hands still tied, made off amongst them. Taking to the paddy fields, he regained Regimental Headquarters to give a clear report on the layout of the Japanese defences.

The Regiment carried out a fighting withdrawal in their reliable Honey light tanks from Rangoon to Schwegyin, a distance of some 480 miles. There, with no heavy ferries with which to cross the River Chindwin, all but one of the tanks had to be destroyed. However, some of the load-carrying vehicles were got across the river and our drivers put up a sterling performance ferrying supplies and men back to Assam. The remaining 140 miles out of Burma were covered mainly on foot. However, unlike our forerunners 134 years earlier in the withdrawal to Corunna, discipline and morale never wavered. How better to conclude this short account than to quote the Commander of the Army in Burma, General, later Field-Marshal The Earl, Alexander "Without the 7th Armoured Brigade we should not have got the army out of Burma."

El Alamein 1942

by Lieutenant-Colonel A G C W Peck, OBE
whose father was killed in the battle while Second-in-Command

The 3rd Hussars formed part of the 9th Armoured Brigade, commanded by Brigadier John Currie. The Brigade was under the command of General Freyberg's 2nd New Zealand Division.

In the opening phase of the battle, the break in, the Regiment supported the attack on the Miteirya Ridge being in action from the night of the 23 October until late on the 27th when the New Zealand Division was withdrawn. Casualties were severe in equipment and personnel, especially among the officers. Early on the 27th Captain Tom Chadwick set out with two other officers, one the Regimental Medical Officer, to find the grave, and make sure it was marked, of his brother Hector who had been killed two days before. The brothers had been devoted and had become something of an institution in the Regiment. Both were excellent soldiers, and Tom was a talented painter, a poet and a humourist. The scout car in which the party was travelling was hit by an 88 mm at close range and all were killed. It was tragic that these lives should be lost, and only for sentiment.

The Regiment was next in action at the climax of the battle. Their task was to exploit beyond the infantry objectives, so that the strong enemy defences in the area of the Sidi Rahman track would be destroyed or taken. When the Commanding Officer, Lieutenant-Colonel Sir Peter Farquhar, was told what it was he was being asked to do he suggested to General Montgomery it was a suicidal task. The 8th Army Commander replied, "It's got to be done and, if necessary, I am prepared to accept 100 per cent casualties in both personnel and tanks". Sir Peter has said, "I have always admired Montgomery for this frank reply – tough but typical of him. There was, of course, no more to be said."

The Regiment lost 10 of their 33 tanks before they reached the infantry objective. The final attack began late and as "A" and "B" Squadrons reached the Rahman track they were silhouetted against the dawn and came under heavy fire at close range from the front and both flanks. Brigadier Lucas Phillips described the battlefield on the morning of 2 November as Brigadier John Currie saw it:

> 'All that could be seen was a world of devastation – devastation of the enemy, indeed, their shattered guns sprawling at crazed angles, their detachments lying dead, but devastation of his own brigade also. As far as the eye could see lay the terrible record – tank after tank burning or wrecked, the smoke of their burning mingled with the cold mist, the crimson shafts from the eastern sky tincturing all objects with the hue of blood. Only here and there could be seen a tank still defiantly shooting it out with the more distant guns and tanks of the Afrika Korps.'

The 3rd learned afterwards they had knocked out 15 anti-tank guns, 4 field guns and 5 tanks, and taken 300 prisoners in this phase of the battle. Later that day the bag was increased by another 88 mm gun and three tanks.

The next morning the three surviving Crusaders of "A" Squadron were sent forward to observe the enemy. General Freyberg drove up with Sir Peter Farquhar and climbed on to the leading tank. The General suddenly exclaimed to the Colonel, "Your Regiment is magnificent! The Hun is beaten – it is now the pursuit."

The fighting was over for the 3rd Hussars on the evening of 3 November. Their total casualties in the twelve days since 23 October when the battle began were 21 officers and 98 soldiers killed, wounded and missing; and out of 51 tanks taken into action 47 had been destroyed. In the words of Major-General John Strawson, himself a distinguished cavalryman and an eminent military historian, the conduct of the 3rd Hussars was exemplary and in the best traditions both of the Regiment itself and the cavalry as a whole.

Ever since this battle, the 3rd Hussars, and now The Queen's Own Hussars, carry the emblem of a fernleaf on their vehicles to commemorate the association with the 2nd New Zealand Division.

It is difficult to grow the New Zealand fernleaf in the United Kingdom, but just possible in the South-West. Lieutenant Colonel W G Petherick, who commanded the 3rd Hussars in the early campaigns in the Desert, has succeeded in growing the fernleaf in his garden near St. Austell in Cornwall.

It is pleasant to record that the association between the Warwickshire Yeomanry and the 3rd Hussars, cemented at the Battle of El Alamein when they served together in 9th Armoured Brigade, started in the year of the raising of the Yeomanry. Then a Troop of the 3rd Hussars worked with them and in January 1795 the Yeomanry presented Cornet John Manley with a silver cup inscribed "in gratitude for his services and attention in training them".

Citta della Pieve – Citta di Castello – Italy 1944

by Colonel A H N Reade, LVO, then Recce Troop Leader, 3rd Hussars

The battle honour of Citta della Pieve was awarded to the 3rd Hussars in recognition of a skilful and determined advance during five days in June 1944 against a highly professional rearguard action fought by a German parachute division. We were attached to 78 Infantry Division, who had problems keeping up, but, as always, the support given by Chestnut Troop, RHA, was magnificent and Major Marcus Linton, the Battery Commander, and his Forward Observation Officers were always up with the leading tank troops. During this period the Regiment advanced some 50 miles, through close, hilly country, doing great damage to the enemy. On one day alone over 200 enemy soft vehicles and many anti-tank guns were destroyed. This success was the result of the long months of training under the inspiring leadership of Lieutenant-Colonel Sir Peter Farquhar. No words of mine can possibly do justice to the debt that the Regiment owed him. After El Alamein he reformed and trained us to the highest standard of efficiency and when we went into battle in Italy his eye for ground and his tactical sense were only equalled by his determination to attack the enemy and his firm resolve that no one in the Regiment would ever be launched into a foolish or ill considered action. One knew one was always in with a good chance and his voice over the air dispelled apprehension and invariably inspired confidence.

On 14 June "C" Squadron, with RHQ and "A" close behind, advanced 19 miles. I caught up with them in the late afternoon, when the leading tank had been knocked out. From a safe distance on the crest behind I was astonished and delighted to spot a 75 mm anti-tank gun beside a haystack some 800 yards ahead and announced my optimistic intention of engaging it with all the devastating fire-power of the Bren Gun in my Scout Car. Immediately Douglas Scott, the Second-in-Command, came up with "Yes, I know. I've been watching that xxxxxx thing for 10 minutes and I'm xxxxxx well going to shoot at it – Now". The Colonel and Adjutant were standing in the road immediately in front of his tank and just got out of the way in time, though the Adjutant's beret was blown off. The next day "A" Squadron led and that night "B" were ordered to take over next morning. However a canal had to be crossed first. For once the Recce Troop was used in what we considered a proper role – to spread out at first light over as wide a front as possible and find a way over. This we did and the Sherman troops of "B" Squadron passed through and fought a copybook action against a brave and skilful defence, entering the outskirts of Citta della Pieve at the end of a very long, hot day. On 17 June "C" Squadron had a difficult time in the narrow streets without proper infantry support and we were then pulled out for two days welcome rest. It bucketed down with rain but we hardly noticed. A month later Peter Farquhar's tactical genius and mastery of ground were again shown when the 3rd Hussars captured the strongly held town of Citta di Castello.

Ancona – Rimini Line – Italy 1944–1945

by General Sir Patrick Howard Dobson, GCB
then 4th Troop Leader, "A" Squadron, 7th Hussars

The importance of Ancona, a town on the east coast of Italy, "the calf", lay in its value as a port; if it could be captured and its docks opened to shipping this would shorten and simplify the supply lines which were by now – mid-summer 1944 – getting long and tenuous. 2nd Polish Corps, which the 7th Hussars joined in mid-June, were therefore ordered to secure the port as soon as possible.

This was easier said than done; the grain of the country was in favour of the defender, as all the rivers and streams ran west/east and each ridge between had to be fought for. Nevertheless, by early July the Corps had reached the enemy's last line of defence before Ancona; the Regiment had come to like the Poles as comrades and to admire their qualities as soldiers, and in the preliminary battles round Loreto, Castelfidardo (known to most of us as "Casselfirkin") and Osimo we had gained confidence in ourselves – we had had a long lay-off since Burma.

We lay in squadron leaguers from 7 to 14 July; the weather was good and we were comfortable enough, but we soon got bored. We then had a long march on the night 14/15 July; this was tedious because we followed steep and winding roads, but it was worth it if it deceived the enemy as to where the armour was. I remember sitting on top of my tank singing "O God our help in ages past" which seemed appropriate at the time.

The plan worked; on the morning of the 17th "A" and "C" Squadrons attacked and secured our first objective, Monte Torto, without difficulty, but the second, Monte Bogo, took the rest of the day. By next morning the infantry divisions had got their objectives, and Colonel Bobinski, second-in-command of the Polish Armoured Brigade, was able to lead the left hook, on which the Corps Commander had based his plan. The Colonel led in his tank; finding this too slow he changed it for a jeep and pressed on. Ancona was in our hands that day; and on the 22nd I was privileged to command a composite troop in a parade in the port to celebrate the victory. General Leese, 8th Army Commander, called it "One of the best small battles the 8th Army had fought" – and we felt ten feet tall.

Two months later the 7th Hussars were again involved in heavy fighting for which they were awarded the battle honour "Rimini Line".

Editor's Note. Captain P J Howard Dobson was awarded, subsequently, the Virtuti Militari – the highest Polish medal for valour.

CHAPTER THREE

More Recent History
Operations since 1945

Since 1945 the British Army has been involved in about 70 separate operations around the world, the exact numbers depending on the definition of what constitutes an operation. Almost all have involved violence, although a few, sometimes the most risky, were able to be prevented by prompt and efficient action. The degree of violence ranged from the full-scale conventional war of Korea to peacekeeping with the United Nations.

The Regiment has been involved in three of these operations:

1. The 3rd Hussars in Palestine 1945–1948.
2. The Queen's Own Hussars in the withdrawal from Aden 1967.
3. The Queen's Own Hussars in three regimental tours in Northern Ireland.

In addition, "C" Squadron were in South Arabia in 1960, "B" Squadron in Cyprus with the United Nations in 1969, and RHQ and "A" Squadron in Northern Ireland in 1972.

In many of the 70 operations Queen's Own Hussars have served as individuals. Most notable were the reinforcements that were supplied to regiments in Korea: a total of 11, of whom one died in captivity and two were wounded.

The following awards were made:

Military Cross	Lieutenant J B Venner
Military Medal	Corporal (A/Sgt) A J G Wallace
Mention in Despatches	Lieutenant K G I Hart
C-in-C's Commendation	Lance-Corporal Kelly

The citation for Corporal Wallace's MM gives some idea of the ferocity of the engagements:

> 'During the period under review A/Sgt Wallace has proved himself to be a fearless leader of men, aggressive in the extreme and with a complete disregard of his personal safety. He distinguished himself particularly in the attack on the Hook at the end of May, when in command of the searchlight tank in the area of Pt 121. For several days and nights prior to the attack he rendered invaluable aid to the infantry with his light and fire and was subjected to a personal bombardment by the enemy in an endeavour to knock him out, during which his tank was hit on several occasions. On the night of the main attack he was

the first into action with his light and fire on the Ronson feature and succeeded in forcing the enemy off the southern slopes, until receiving three direct hits which destroyed his light and machine gun. Later he fitted a spare machine gun which entailed considerable movement and exposure on his part outside the tank under shelling and mortaring.

'He was the first to detect and engage the enemy probe on the Pioneer platoon position and coolly directed his own fire, plus that of another tank on to the enemy who were then in the wire and subjecting him to "burp" gun fire.

'Later he detected movement in the Betty Grable – Seattle area and by intelligent use of his own fire and wireless sets, was able to direct the fire of other tanks and his infantry platoon on to the target area, successfully keeping the enemy pinned until the more normal forms of defensive fire could be brought down. During this action his loader was seriously affected by fumes and became a passenger, so determined was this NCO to keep his tank in action that he took over these duties in addition to his own. By his determination he kept his tank in continuous action for a period of over eight hours and displayed outstanding devotion to duty'.

Staff Sergeants are addressed as "Sergeant Major" because they used to be Troop Sergeant Majors.

The modern Trooper might applaud the "Standing Orders to be Observed by the Whole Corps of Dragoons": "As a Sergeant Major is a new thing in the Dragoons (being introduced by lazy Adjutants) it is forbid in the future". This clearly has not happened!
"No Dragoon shall be made a Corporal merely because he can write a good hand, as has been hitherto the Custom ... the Non-commissioned Officers will be compleat Soldiers and not simple Scribblers."

ISSUED BY HRH THE DUKE OF CUMBERLAND,
COMMANDER-IN-CHIEF 1755

"Personal Maintenance". "B" Squadron, 7th Hussars. Early Desert

(above)
The Battle of Moodkee. 18 December 1845
E Croft
From a painting in the Officers' Mess

(left)
The Light Camel Corps. 1884–1885
Harry Payne
From an illustration in "The 7th (Queen's Own) Hussars", by C R B Barrett

In 1884 an expedition was assembled in Egypt to try to relieve General Gordon, stranded in Khartoum. The expedition included a Camel Corps, for which both the 3rd and 7th Hussars provided detachments of 2 officers and 44 other ranks for the Light Camel Regiment. The Commanding Officer, a 7th Hussar, commented 'If you ever want to know the pleasure of being on a horse, just try 1,000 miles on a camel.' It seems, however, that the camelmastership may have been weak: out of 7,000 camels, 4,000 were left to rot in the desert.

The Battle of Chillianwallah. 13th June 1849
Henry Martens
From a painting in the possession of Captain T Unett
(Served in the 3rd Hussars 1950–1958)

Captain T Unett supplied the following abridged version of the description of the scene.

   The Painting represents the situation when the Squadron, having charged through the Sikhs, had reformed and started to charge back to regain their own lines. Many Sikhs were carried with the Squadron in the initial charge and they are now intermingled. In the centre of the painting is Captain W Unett, the Squadron Leader, who has received a sword cut across his back, the force of the blow being in part turned by the buckle of the despatch box which it cut in two. The Sikh who inflicted the blow was cut down by Trooper Fetch. To the left is a Sikh lancer who charged at Captain Unett, but was felled by Trooper Todd whose sword broke on the man's head. Sergeant McGaskill is on the ground in front. His wounds left him crippled. Just above him and to the right is Sergeant Thomson, last seen defending himself with a double-barreled pistol. To his left is young Trooper Milligan thrusting his sword into a Sikh. The wounded man, by a desperate effort, decapitated Milligan with a back-hand blow. Bottom right is Farrier Johnson whose faithful dog followed the charge and stayed with the body for two days until it was buried. Lieutenant Stisted is in the centre background. It is believed that he, like Captain Unett, came from a Birmingham family.

"A" Squadron, 3rd Hussars. Tidworth. 1936

Mk VI Light Tank. Issued to the 3rd Hussars. 1938

The 7th Hussars Drumhorse. 1876   *B Cam Norton*
From a painting in the possession of James Bouskell Esq, MFH (Served in "A" Squadron, 7th Hussars 1954–1956)

    The date "1876" may be misleading. The Regimental Records show that in the first half of the year the Regiment was dispersed between Norwich and Liverpool, concentrating in the second half in the Edinburgh area. However, in July 1874 the Regiment had concentrated at Aldershot under canvas for "the summer drills". In August there is a specific mention of the Band. It is possible that the artist made a sketch during the Summer of 1874, but did not complete the oil painting until 1876.

Palestine

by Major General A M L Hogge, CB
then 2nd Troop Leader, "A" Squadron, 3rd Hussars

The Regiment arrived in Palestine in October 1945 after a year in Lebanon and Syria following service in Italy. Stationed initially some 12 miles south-east of the Jewish city of Tel Aviv, within four months the Regiment became part of the 6th Airborne Division and absorbed some 400 of us on the disbandment of the Division's Armoured Reconnaissance Regiment and 20th and 22nd Independent Parachute Companies. Four moves and 2½ years later we were to return home after a most varied and contrasting life in a fascinating country sadly rent by political divides.

The task was to keep the peace between Arab and Jew and to limit Jewish immigration from Europe while protecting ourselves against illegal Jewish armed organisations. From the autumn of 1947 when the end of the British Mandate was announced and the United Nations agreed to partition, the tempo of operations increased as the Jews attempted to drive us out of "their homeland" while the Arabs strove to retain such land as was their due.

"Showing the Flag", curfew patrols, escorting VIPs and command cashiers, and the protection of oil refineries were day to day tasks in our Staghound armoured cars, coupled to incessant mounted and dismounted guards. Operations with the Palestine Police involved the cordoning and searching of settlements and towns including the four day long curfew and search of Tel Aviv for suspects and arms. This operation, during which my troop supposedly resting between patrols discovered an arms cache in the school which was our base, followed the blowing up of the King David Hotel in Jerusalem in 1946.

During quiet periods opportunities were seized to visit other Middle East countries, and to train in all aspects of armoured car work while maintaining operational readiness. This once entailed our Squadron making a successful 2 am "flap" move back from the Dead Sea despite a preceding "squadron smoker". Parachute training took place regularly and some 350 of us so qualified. Many forms of sport, including shooting snipe and duck, provided welcome relaxation.

Early in 1948 the Arab Liberation Army started operations and the long years of battle between Arab and Jew began once more. Now stationed on the Plain of Esdraelon with a squadron on Mount Carmel, our major area of interest was Haifa. Communal strife, arson, road mining and sniping continued. At times Haifa assumed an air of war and our Staghounds had to be protected for road block busting by welding railway lines across their hulls.

For the withdrawal to Egypt in May 1948 we were the divisional rear guard and so were the last British troops to cross the frontier where we met the "invading" Egyptian Army patiently awaiting our departure. We sailed home to be welcomed by the 7th Hussars at Barnard Castle before moving to BAOR. No one could then foretell that 10 years later the two Regiments were to become one, and that 19 years later the Regiment would be on operations once more in armoured cars and with a parachute battalion, this time in Aden.

We were relieved to leave Palestine yet the total experience left a lasting impression. The hospitality of the Arabs, the drive and innovation of the Jews, the scenery, the splendid climate, and the many places of historical interest will all be remembered.

The 3rd Hussars were no strangers to keeping the peace in the Eastern Mediterranean. In 1921 the Regiment left Aldershot to join the Allied Army of Occupation in Turkey. They were stationed initially at Soghanli on the Asiatic shore of the Bosphorus. Life was pleasant with exchange visits to the Royal Navy in the Sea of Marmara and hunting foxes, jackals, and even wolves with "The Anatolian Hounds". In the summer of 1922 the Regiment entertained almost the entire British Colony of Constantinople at their regimental sports.

This amiable pattern, however, was broken in July 1922 when the Greeks, fearing the Turks, demanded permission to enter Constantinople from Thrace. "B" Squadron, on the European side, were hurriedly reinforced by the rest of the Regiment, ferried across the Bosphorus. No sooner were the Greeks dissuaded from their plan than the Turks, sweeping the Greeks into the sea at Smyrna, advanced North on Constantinople. The Regiment were ferried back across the Bosphorus to meet this new threat. In one incident 3,000 Kemalist Cavalry tried to unseat "B" Squadron by seizing their bridles. The situation became so tense that on October 10th the British Government authorised fire to be opened the following day. With only 75 minutes to spare, an armistice was signed. The 3rd Hussars left for Egypt in August 1923.

Aden – 1967

by Colonel J B Venner MC
then "A" Squadron Leader

The Palace of the Sultan of Lahej, the Queen of Sheba's Wells, the Tower of Silence, Sabeel Street – evocative and romantic names, recalling fading memories of a squadron tour in that most prosaic of districts – Crater. We were there to support The Argyll & Sutherland Highlanders, who a few weeks earlier had erupted onto the floor of that extinct volcano.

When the order comes to go abroad unaccompanied on an exciting operation of limited duration, with a sporting chance of being shot at, a duty to fire back, and most of the odds against being killed, the family farewells bear ill-disguised words of parting sorrow. A few hours by air from our Sussex camp, a touchdown in Tehran, and we were in the country of sand, blue seas, petro-storage terminals and oil-soaked pelicans, with that pungent all-pervading heat of an eastern port.

How well the men of Birmingham deported themselves in Crater! Perhaps being bred in a city makes for a certain affinity with urban soldiering. We patrolled for one hour on, one hour off for up to 15 hours a day in fairly dreadful conditions; so hot were the road surfaces and so much street driving did the Saladin armoured cars perform, that tyres had to be changed weekly. We helped to keep the NLF away from FLOSY (Front for the Liberation of South Yemen) and FLOSY away from the NLF, and both of them away from us and the bewildered population for some five months, so that the transition to independence could be smooth and seem honourable. Towards the end, we extended our activities to Maalla and the waterfront in support of 45 Commando, Royal Marines. We left, some by air, some on HMS *Intrepid* to Dubai, and some via the Cape on RFA *Sir Galahad* – later ill-fated off the Falkland Islands.

It was all a long time ago: a soldier joining the Regiment in our tercentenary year was only a babe in arms at the time. The great thing about having served in such a place is that thereafter one follows the progress and tribulations of that country with keen interest. What gives in Aden now? Well, the ... (*No more space. Ed.*)

Northern Ireland

by Colonel R D H H Greenwood
Commanding Officer 1976–1979

In 1972, after an absence from Ireland of 93 years, and at the end of the first year the Regiment had spent together since 1964, RHQ and "A" Squadron were sent to County Armagh. This was the first of four tours that the Regiment was to undertake from BAOR in the 1970s.

"A" Squadron were deployed in the traditional light reconnaissance role and were mounted in Ferret scout cars. Unusually RHQ did not command "A" Squadron, the units placed under their command were sub-units of the Royal Scots Dragoon Guards, the 7th Regiment Royal Horse Artillery and the 1st Battalion the Devon and Dorset Regiment. The tours of both RHQ and "A" Squadron were described as relatively quiet but successful. They undoubtedly did much to reassure local communities. RHQ's particular experience in Newry led to the comment "Crater (Aden) and Newry are remarkably similar at times, both in their scruffy appearance and the behaviour of some of their inhabitants".

Little over a year later, Lieutenant Colonel J B Venner, MC, returned to Ulster for his second tour as Commanding Officer, but this time taking with him the whole Regiment; the first cavalry Regiment to go to Northern Ireland complete in the infantry role. The Regiment were deployed in Belfast, and it was my good fortune to be the Squadron Leader of "A" Squadron in south-west Belfast, where we experienced what was probably the most interesting and action-packed tour of any Queen's Own Hussar Squadron in Ulster's current troubled times.

Military service in Ireland has often been described as the Section Commanders (Tank Commanders) and Squadron or Company Commanders war. My own experience, for I was later to command a regiment in the theatre, leads me to share this view, although I should add that the freedom and scope for operational initiative and opportunism that were open to sub-unit commanders in urban Belfast in 1973 were vastly different to those which pertained when I commanded the Regiment in Ireland four years later.

In June 1973, after two hectic months of learning the rigours and skills of the infantry soldier, "A" Squadron relieved two companies of the 1st Battalion Cheshire Regiment and set up their operational base in the bombed-out/burned-out ruins of the Woodburn Hotel, Suffolk, Belfast. The Squadron's peace-keeping tasks included policing an ultra-sensitive Protestant/Catholic interface, to which the RUC could not at that time be effective (or indeed present), patrolling in an endeavour to reassure, and generally getting to know the people. The area was relatively small with the result that the soldiers quickly learned who was who, who could be trusted and who could not. The intimidation aspect was very serious, for at this time the Catholic community were endeavouring to set up homes in the area, whilst the Protestants sought to keep them out.

Both sides deployed much the same tactics, ie they used their thug elements to scare the wits out of the minority groups, particularly in the mixed areas of the local housing estates, (not a difficult task if blind shooting through doors and setting houses on fire are the tools of persuasion). This was normally done as a prelude to illegal squatting, from which in Belfast at that time followed the right to the legal occupancy of the houses concerned. It presented a difficult problem, nonetheless "A" Squadron found an answer. This was to move men of the Squadron into the vacant houses as they became empty and before the illegals could get there, when families decided to move away to safer areas. Such occupation by the soldiers lasted until the housing executive could move legal occupiers into the houses in question. It stretched manpower resources at times but it worked most successfully.

This tour was also marked by the fact that the Squadron experienced at least one of each type of incident for which it had been trained. For example, a major and a minor riot, a rocket attack against the base, a successful ambush (laid on by us!), the experience of being shot at and bombed against etc etc. In all these cases our local knowledge, speedy reaction and good fortune stood the Squadron in good stead.

In 1977 I commanded three squadrons of the Regiment, a squadron of Life Guards and a company of the 1st Battalion the Black Watch, all operating in the infantry role, but in County Armagh. We were responsible for 550 square miles of Northern Ireland, including many miles of border and countless crossing places. The activities of the squadrons were numerous and varied, ranging from the normal heavy load of foot patrols in Armagh City, helicopter operations and escort duties to the very discrete and lengthy close observation tasks. There is no doubt that during this tour the Regiment did much to help in the build-up of the intelligence picture particularly concerning the on-the-run terrorists who made forays into our area from the south; nonetheless it was desperately sad that whilst we were there, three RUC constables were ambushed and murdered in their car, whilst later, and in separate incidents, three members of the UDR (two UDR battalions were in our area) were similarly murdered.

The termination of this tour marked yet a further achievement, of which the Regiment was justifiably proud. At the end of our tour in Belfast in 1973 The Queen's Own Hussars was the first major unit in the Army to achieve no negligent discharges during a Northern Ireland tour. This achievement was repeated in 1977.

I will end with a quotation from a letter written by our Brigade Commander in 1977:

> 'We shall miss the light cavalry style in mid-Ulster – which is the "no hassle" approach, getting the job done thoroughly and efficiently without making a noise about it'.

A fair tribute, I believe, to the troopers, NCOs, warrant officers and officers of The Queen's Own Hussars.

Editor's Note. Colonel Greenwood was awarded a mention in despatches for his tour as "A" Squadron Leader.

CHAPTER FOUR

The Famous – The Eccentric – The Unorthodox

The Regiment has always had more than its share of the famous, the eccentric, and the unorthodox: the arrogant but high-principled first Colonel of the Regiment, the 6th Duke of Somerset; Sir John Cope, the distinguished commander of the second line of cavalry at Dettingen; Sir Stapleton Cotton, judged by the Duke of Wellington to be his best cavalry commander in the Napoleonic Wars; the Marquess of Anglesey, the commander of the cavalry at Waterloo; and Lord Haig, the British Commander-in-Chief in France 1915–1918.

However, three, perhaps lesser-known, personalities have been chosen for this chapter: Major General Gaspard Le Marchant who, had he not been killed at Salamanca, might have proved the finest commander as well as trainer of cavalry of his time; Squire Mytton, if not of particularly edifying character at least one of the greatest eccentrics ever; and the unorthodox General Sir George de Lacy Evans.

This tradition, nevertheless, continues to modern times. Illustrating the famous, the present Chief of the General Staff, General Sir John Stanier, commanded "C" Squadron 1961–1963. Furthermore, the day of the eccentric is certainly not over: the eccentricities and practical jokes of one of the authors in this book had, in his late twenties, led cumulatively to almost as much fortfeiture of seniority as he had earned! He, as so often with eccentrics, proved a gallant soldier, fighting his tank troop with great panache in one of the post-1945 minor wars. In another, he posed his Commanding Officer with the dilemma of whether to recommend a Court Martial for disobedience of at least four operational standing orders or the award of a Military Cross for the single-handed and vigorous pursuit of a group of rebels. In the event, the account was squared off by neither action being taken.

One of the outstanding unorthodox soldiers of the 1939–1945 war was Major Roy Farran, DSO, MC, the author of the article on Crete. More recently the last Commanding Officer, Lieutenant-Colonel Jeremy Phipps, has served two tours with the SAS; but an account of these cannot as yet be published.

Major-General John Gaspard Le Marchant (1766–1812)

by Brigadier D H Davies, MC
Colonel of the Regiment 1965–1969

Most famous commanders are remembered by their great victories on the field of battle, and so might John Le Marchant have been had he not met an untimely death whilst leading the Heavy Brigade in the vital charge that won the day against the French at Salamanca in the Peninsular Campaign. In this famous charge he cut down six of the enemy with his own hand before being mortally wounded by a musket ball in the groin. The year was 1812, three years before Waterloo and he was only "46".

John Le Marchant was born in Amiens in Picardy in 1766 at the family home of his mother, the daughter of a French aristocrat. His father, also "John", was an officer in the 7th Light Dragoons and Scion of an ancient "Guernsey" family, being one of the first Guernseymen to hold a commission in the British Army. Thus it was that in Guernsey young John spent his early and formative years.

He was later educated privately at Dr Morgan's Boarding School at Bath, but he proved too turbulent a pupil, and his father was forced to remove him to continue his education at home, tutored mainly by the family butler, an American loyalist who was unusually well-read. At sixteen, young Le Marchant had had enough of the schoolroom, and was firm in his resolve to become a soldier. His father, due to straitened circumstances, could not afford to purchase a commission for him in his own regiment, so after scouting around managed to buy him a commission in The Wiltshire Militia, which he joined in 1781 as an ensign.

Shortly after joining his regiment he challenged his commanding officer to a duel, and whilst this was smoothed over he later "called out" a civilian and the peace officers had to intervene. This all proved too much and the young "firebrand" was transferred to the 1st Regiment of Foot (The Royal Scots), then stationed in Dublin and under orders to sail for Gibraltar. On the eve of embarkation, young Le Marchant spent his time in a gambling house where he lost £200. There seemed no alternative but to sell out and quit the army. In desperation he approached the regimental pay-master who kindly lent him the money with one condition that he never touched cards again. This promise was faithfully kept and over the years the debt repaid. Thus was his career saved.

He spent some uneventful and boring years in Gibraltar, where, to alleviate the boredom, he took up water colour painting, which he continued all his life, and his work ultimately gained the praise of King George III himself. Still he had no intention of wasting any more time as a junior officer in an infantry of the line regiment, and persuaded his father to buy him a "Cornetcy" in the cavalry. Ultimately he got a commission in the 6th Dragoons or Inniskillings. Later, when the Inniskillings were ordered to provide the King's escort for His Majesty's annual trip to Weymouth, Le Marchant was given the command. From then on he became a firm favourite of the ailing King George III, who quickly sensed that here was an officer of no ordinary calibre.

Early in 1793 Britain slipped into war against revolutionary France, and Le Marchant saw his first active service with the armies in the Netherlands. He served with distinction with his own regiment and later in command of the 2nd Dragoons (The Queen's Bays). His talent was spotted by the Duke of York, the Commander-in-Chief, and on numerous occasions he was called on to serve on the staff. The whole campaign proved a disaster, and Le Marchant observed what was lacking in the training and administration of the army.

Back in England in 1795 and promoted to Major in the 16th Dragoons, he set himself the task of improving the training of the cavalry. He designed a new sword, and it was at Bordesley in Birmingham that he found the right man to help him. He was Henry Osborn, a sword cutler and victualler, who had acquired a local reputation. On the recommendation of the Duke of York the sword was adopted by the Board of Ordnance, and thus gave the army one of the finest cutting weapons ever forged. Le Marchant then wrote a manual for its use "Rules and Regulations for Sword Exercise of the Cavalry", which was published by the War Office to be observed and practised by the Cavalry Corps in general.

In 1797 Le Marchant was summoned to a Levee wearing the uniform of the 16th Dragoons. The King chided him, "How can you be so little of a martinet to appear at Court in the wrong dress?" and laughed heartily at Le Marchant's embarrassment. "You may now wear the 7th Coat", he said, "as I have this morning appointed you Lieutenant-Colonel of the 7th Light Dragoons, and am glad to tell you of it". Thus after so many years he became a member of his father's regiment.

Still in England whilst the army was fighting in Spain and Portugal, he turned his attention to the training of young officers and staff officers, and devoted his active mind and all his energy to this end. It was not easy to convert the very conservative military establishment to his views, particularly in time of war. Still, through his determination and the support of the Duke of York, he succeeded in founding the Royal Military College at Wycombe for the training of young officers, with a class for training staff officers. This small beginning was to result in the Royal Military College, Sandhurst, and the Staff College, Camberley. He was the first Lieutenant-Governor, but sadly did not live to see his efforts come to full fruition. Still today his achievement is as great a memorial as any single victory in battle.

In 1811 he was promoted to Major-General and left England for the last time to join Wellington's Army in the Peninsula. He commanded a cavalry brigade at Ciudad Rodrigo, Llerene, Badajoz, and at Salamanca, where he met a truly gallant end.

Le Marchant was a true cavalryman – a brilliant horseman, and superb swordsman, one of the best of his day. To that rare quality, a stainless honour, was added a fertile original mind and an unusual talent for administration. He was in essence a soldier, artist and author, who was cut off in his prime, when he had a great deal still to offer king and country.

He married early, Mary de la Bigoterie, the daughter of a Guernsey landowner, to whom he was devoted, and who bore him eight children. They all distinguished themselves in their various fields. His eldest son, "Carey", was killed in action shortly after his father in the Battle of the Nive in 1814.

As a tribute to an almost unsung hero a pension of £1,200 pa was voted to his family, and £1,500 was voted by the House of Lords for a statue to be erected to his memory in St Paul's Cathedral.

In 1797 Le Marchant, with Lord Paget (later Marquess of Anglesey) as Colonel, trained the 7th Hussars so hard that nine officers exchanged or resigned. In the summer of 1801, however, King George III reviewed the Regiment and expressed "his royal approbation of their appearance and field movements". The Prince of Wales complimented Le Marchant personally after the parade. "Among many flattering references to the transformation of the Regiment, he added enviously that he wished his own regiment would soon be their equals."

The hard training, however, cannot have involved much field firing. Even by 1814 the annual individual training ammunition allocation for the carbine was only:

>   *10 rounds ball*
>   *20 rounds blank*
>   *1 flint*

John Mytton Esq

by Major J L Damant
"B" Squadron Leader 1963–1965

John Mytton was born on the 30 September 1796 at Halston in Shropshire, heir to a very large estate from the age of two, when his father died. The name Mytton came from the Norman "de Mutton" and his family had lived in Halston from 1373. As a child he was nicknamed "Mango, King of the Pickles" by his neighbour Sir Richard Puleston, and was expelled from both Westminster School and Harrow. It was said that the only indication that he intended to go to University was that he ordered "Three pipes of port" to be sent to him at his address at Cambridge.

At 19 he joined the 7th Hussars who were stationed near Calais with the Army of Occupation after Waterloo, and was quartered at Guines, six miles from Calais. While there, he was involved in many escapades. He borrowed £3,000 from a banker in St Omer and lost half of it in an evening at a "crooked" rouge et noir table which he demolished to atoms as some satisfaction for his loss. He lost 16,000 Napoleons at billiards to a certain captain, and not having come into his inheritance, was unable to pay. The Marquess of Anglesey, Colonel of the Regiment, suspecting a put-up job, forbade him to pay the debt.

In 1818 he left the Regiment to get married, leaving in the mess various pieces of silver, the most famous of which are two silver jugs with Paschal Lamb motifs.

He was apparently a very well built man of about 5 ft 10 ins, with biceps larger than Jackson, the well-known boxer, and he was known as "a very awkward customer in a turn-up", in which he was frequently involved!

His exploits during the period 1818 until his death in 1834 are legendary and are contained in the "Memoirs in the Life of the Late John Mytton Esq" by Nimrod. Briefly his escapades include: wildfowling by moonlight in his nightshirt in freezing weather; driving a rather precious fellow in a gig who asked him to drive more slowly as it was dangerous, and Mytton asked him if he had never been upset. On being told "No", he said, "What a damned slow fellow you must have been all your life!" and promptly ran a wheel up the bank and turned them over. "They were neither much hurt!"

On another occasion he sent a coal merchant to knock on the door of a money-lender every two hours of the night until he had secured a loan. Another jape was to ride into dinner on his pet bear which bit him in the leg for his pains! Having broken the bank in two London gambling "Hells" playing at Hazard, he was counting his winnings while being driven home at night when several thousand pounds blew out of the coach window. "Easy come, easy go", was his only remark on the loss.

He owned many famous horses, including Claudius which won the Gold Cup at Cheltenham in 1821. Although his constitution was of iron, five bottles of port a day (he was said to have been permanently drunk for twelve years), and finally brandy, drained his health and resources.

To escape his creditors he returned to Calais, where he had been quartered with the 7th Hussars, and one of his final acts, when suffering from a bad attack of hiccoughs, was to set fire to the tail of his night-shirt to cure them! Although curing the hiccoughs he was severely burned, and on his return to England was promptly arrested for debts and put into prison in London where he died awaiting trial, at the age of 38.

So popular was he that his funeral at Halston was attended by over 3,000 people, and the cortege was headed by a squadron of the North Shropshire Cavalry, of which he had been a major.

Joshua Guest, probably illegitimate and an ostler, joined the 3rd Hussars as a Trooper in 1685. He served some 50 years in the Regiment, became a Lieutenant General and was buried in Westminster Abbey.

In 1811 John Andrews, commissioned from the ranks and a veteran of Dettingen, attended his last parade – a review by the Prince Regent – at the age of 90. He was wearing an "antique uniform" and riding "an old hack". Seeing him "drest in an old suit of Regimentals" the Prince asked how long he had worn them. "Why, your Royal Highness, about 40 years" was the reply. The Prince, feeling the texture of the coat, commented "such cloth was not made nowadays". "No," replied Andrews, "nor such men neither". This reply so pleased the Prince that Andrews was restored from half to full pay.

General Sir George De Lacy Evans

by Colonel H M Sandars
Commanding Officer 1979–1982

George De Lacy Evans was born in 1787. He joined the Army in India in 1806, as a volunteer, and was commissioned in 1807 in the 22nd (Cheshire) Regiment. He first saw action the same year against the Amir Khan and the Pindaris. He was again in action in 1808 in the capture of Mauritius from the French and was promoted to Lieutenant for his services. Seeing further active service, he transferred in 1812 to the 3rd King's Own Dragoons, then serving in the Peninsula.

He took part with the Regiment in a number of Peninsular battles, among them Vittoria and Toulouse, during which he was wounded and had two horses shot from under him. From 1814 he served in the United States. He took part in the Battle of Blankenburg, where he again had two horses killed; and seized the Congress House in Washington with only 200 men. Finally, he took part in Naval Operations before New Orleans, where he was the only Army Officer to receive the Naval General Service Medal for his action.

He returned to Europe in time to rejoin Wellington's army for Quatre Bras. At Waterloo he again had two horses killed (making a total of six). He was promoted to Captain in January 1815 for his Peninsular services, Brevet Major in May 1815 for the American War, and Brevet Lieutenant Colonel for Waterloo in June 1815: three promotions in six months.

He returned on half-pay in 1818, and was elected to Parliament in 1830. He commanded the British Legion of 10,000 men in Spain during the Carlist War 1835–1836, for which he was made a KCB and awarded the Orders of St Ferdinand and Charles III.

After a further period of retirement and as a member of Parliament he returned to active service for the Crimea as a Lieutenant General in 1852. He commanded the 2nd Division at Alma, and at Sebastopol where he was again wounded. On hearing the sound of guns, he discharged himself from the hospital ship to take part in the Battle of Inkerman. For these services he was made a GCB and received the Legion of Honour, the Turkish Order of Medjidie and a presentation sword from Hythe, Folkestone and Sandgate.

He was promoted to full General in 1861 and died in 1870 aged 82. His medals are in the Regimental Museum.

Samuel Russell, Cornet, 7th Dragoons. *c.* 1770   *Circle of Miller*   From a painting in the Regimental Museum
It is believed that this picture was painted at his home in Worcestershire. If this is so, it is the earliest known painting of a scene in the present recruiting area of the Regiment.

The 7th Hussars' Last Mounted Parade. 5 March 1936
Both photographs were taken at "Virgin's Breasts" near Abbassia Barracks, Cairo

The 7th Hussars' First Mechanised Parade. 2 March 1937

"Boots and Saddle". A 7th Hussar *c.* 1813
Artist unknown
From a painting in the Warrant Officers' and Sergeants' Mess

CHAPTER FIVE

Dress Distinctions

by Major N R Haines
Second-in-Command 1983–1984

At first glance it may appear, now, that a sartorial division was made at the time of amalgamation between the "Blue" uniforms which followed the tradition of the 3rd Hussars and the "Drab" uniforms which followed those of the 7th. I do not think any conscious effort was made to this effect, it must just have seemed the most obvious thing to do. The 3rd had spent the post-war years in Europe and were accustomed to temperate Mess Dress and Blue Patrols, the 7th had not long returned from the Far East where "Jungle Green" was the normal order and white was worn for "Best".

In the early part of the 19th century when Hussar-style uniforms were first introduced into the British Army, and indeed throughout their existence, the patterns in all the regiments were the same. Regiments were distinguished one from another by small differences of colour only in so much as affected busby plumes, busby bags, some collars and, in the case of the 11th, their trousers. The only exception to this was in the patrol jacket. They were all dark blue throughout but trimmed with black lambswool and braided with black mohair. The patterns for trimming and braiding were distinctly different for each regiment.

It is remarkable, then, that the scarlet collar of the 3rd Hussars is perpetuated in the "Blue" uniforms of The Queen's Own Hussars. Commonplace abroad, the scarlet collar is unique among British Hussar regiments although in the army as a whole, the 9th Lancers had a scarlet collar as does the Royal Horse Artillery. Bands of the Royal Marines also wear a scarlet collar to their full dress tunics which are blue. Some like to say that it is worn in recognition of the large proportion of the regiment which died from neck wounds at Dettingen but I think that unlikely as Bland's Dragoons wore scarlet frocks with garter blue facings for many years afterwards.

One of the extreme measures to emphasize the concept of light cavalry at its inception as opposed to heavy cavalry, was the use of "Ball" buttons. The idea that an Hussar should ride as light as possible gave rise to the theory that, were he to run short of ammunition in combat, ball buttons could be broken off at the shank and loaded into pistol or carbine. The half ball buttons worn in the regiment today would not suit, of course, because they are hollow but their smooth surface serves as a reminder of the original idea.

Few regiments in the Army can incorporate the garter in their insignia and it should be seen as a privilege, originally of the 3rd Hussars, which is perpetuated in the crest and officers' cap badge of The Queen's Own Hussars. The distinctive colour of the garter sash is also used to back the officers' badges of rank and the non commissioned officers' arm badges. The authorised facing colour of "Garter Blue" is a much darker shade and is the colour of the robes of that order as can be seen in the older paintings of the scarlet frocked dragoons.

Shoulder chains are worn in blue patrol jackets throughout the cavalry of the line and are reminiscent of the Sikh Wars. It was found that the troopers (who frequently did battle in their stable jackets or blue serge frocks to escape the heat of full dress jackets) suffered a high proportion of neck and shoulder wounds from the sweeping cuts of the Sikhs' great curved swords and shoulder chains were introduced to reduce this effect. The blue patrol jacket of today is, in fact, much more the successor of the blue serge frock than of the patrol jackets of the 19th century and that is how shoulder chains have remained with us to the present.

The drab or khaki uniforms began to appear at the end of the last century in India as a measure of camouflage. This was accelerated in South Africa but at each interval of peace, every effort is made to embellish or even beautify these originally practical garments. Again, officers' badges of rank and non commissioned officers' arm badges are backed with the same pale blue. The soldiers' collar badges are backed with scarlet in recognition of the scarlet collars of the blue uniforms, although the officers' collar badges, in silver, gilt and enamel, do not appear to need it.

In service dress, every man in the Regiment wears the badge of the 2nd Polish Corps on his left arm in the pattern of the one presented to the 7th Hussars by General Anders to mark the close association of that regiment with the Corps during the Adriatic Campaign in Italy in 1944.

The officers' service dress jacket is unique in the Army today as its whole back is cut from one piece of cloth without any seams. Officers' also wear "turn ups" on their service dress slacks in common with several other cavalry regiments, presumably to emphasize the fact that they are slacks and not breeches or overalls which a horseman, and therefore a cavalry officer, might normally be expected to wear.

As many of the distinctions of service dress as were applicable were also worn on battle dress whilst it was issued. Officers could have "turn ups" on their slacks and all ranks wore the Polish Badge on their left arm. Badges of rank, however, were embroidered with brown and white thread onto khaki worsted cloth which, in turn, was felled onto the blouse. Battle dress ceased to be issued generally in the early 1960's and, as far as dress for the field is concerned, it was replaced by combat dress, a smock and trousers of olive green to start with but replaced by a disrupted camouflage pattern in the early 1970's.

Although divisional and brigade flashes have been worn on the upper arm in combat dress and, also, flashes bearing the wearer's name over the left breast were ordered for a while, no distinctions are worn in combat dress now except for embroidered badges of rank and, for the officers only, embroidered regimental shoulder titles.

Unusual Orders, Decorations and Medals

by Major R C McDuell
Served in the Regiment 1949–1968

Orders, decorations and medals fall broadly into four categories: those awarded for gallantry, those for distinguished service, those for long and meritorious service and those reflecting the individual's presence at a specific action or participation in a particular campaign. Awards for gallantry, for distinguished and for long and meritorious service are recorded in publications such as the London Gazette, whilst an individual's entitlement to a Campaign Medal or a specific bar to a Campaign Medal is reflected in the various medal rolls drawn up in meticulous fashion by generations of orderly room sergeants.

However, of particular interest is the award such as a Campaign Medal to which an individual or a small group of individuals is entitled, but for which the Regiment as a whole did not qualify. Insofar as The Queen's Own Hussars are concerned the most important of these individuals must be General Sir George de Lacy Evans, GCB. De Lacy Evans whilst a 3rd Light Dragoon received the Bar for the Pyrenees to his Military General Service Medal, the only member of the Regiment to do so, but far more unique is his entitlement to the Naval General Service Medal with the Bar for Boat Service 14 December 1814. He had taken part in the Battle of Blandensburg, had seized the Congress in Washington with only 200 men and had been present at the attack on Baltimore. In the naval operations before New Orleans he was the only army officer to receive the NGS for this action.

The first unique group of individuals is that party of recruits under Cornet Colt, which whilst on its way to join the 3rd Light Dragoons in January 1846, fought alongside the 16th Lancers at Aliwal, for which action it received the Sutlej Medal. Again, whilst neither Regiment served in the Crimea at least one 3rd Light Dragoon and one 7th Hussar received the medal for that campaign.

During the campaigns in Egypt in the 1880's Lieutenant Patton of the 3rd Hussars and Lieutenant Mynors of the 7th Hussars fought with the 4th Dragoon Guards at Tel El Kebir; Patton was to die of enteric in India shortly before the Regiment left for the South African War in 1901. Major Phipps of the 7th Hussars also received the Nile Medal with the Bars for Abu Klea and the Nile 1884–1885, but of rather more interest is the fact that this officer had in 1872 received the Royal Humane Society's Medal in bronze for rescuing a soldier of the 3rd Dragoon Guards who was in danger of drowning whilst on manoeuvres. Neither Regiment took part in this campaign, but both provided detachments for the Light Camel Regiment comprising two officers, four warrant officers and sergeants, one trumpeter and 36 privates all of whom received the Egypt Medal with the Bar Nile 1884–1885. When some years later the 21st Lancers were despatched from England for the Sudan Campaign they were accompanied by "B" Squadron of the 3rd Hussars. The latter, however, did not participate in the campaign although one soldier of the Regiment, Private R J Spratt, did accompany the 21st Lancers and subsequently received the medal.

Both Regiments served in the latter stages of the South African War, neither qualifying as units for the King's South Africa Medal. However, small numbers from both Regiments received the medal having been called up as reservists in the early stages of the war and sent to South Africa to serve with other regiments or with Remount Depots and Town Guards. Four 3rd Hussars, Sergeants Lance and Longman and Privates Hayward and Low served during the early stages of the war with Lumsden's Horse and of these the last three returned to gain additional bars with the Regiment. From the 7th Hussars Privates Aylen and Burditt, in addition to gaining those bars for which the Regiment qualified, also received that for Rhodesia having served with the Rhodesian Field Force.

On the outbreak of the Great War in August 1914 Captain Cross of the 7th Hussars accompanied the 3rd Hussars to France and later that year was to be wounded and mentioned in despatches with the Regiment. Although the 7th Hussars did not leave India until 1917 a number of their reservists were recalled to the colours on the outbreak of war and served in France with the Household Cavalry Regiment. However, in spite of the fact that they did not reach Mesopotamia until 1917 the 7th can count amongst its medals some unique awards. It received one of the very few Meritorious Service Medals awarded for bravery, whilst Sergeants Bennett and Wagstaff received the same medal "in recognition of valuable services rendered in connection with Military Operations in north and north-east Persia during the period 1917–1921". Finally, four sergeants of the 7th Hussars were to be the only British other ranks to receive the newly created General Service Medal with the Bar for South Persia whilst serving with the locally raised unit The South Persia Rifles.

There are no doubt other individuals from both Regiments who served in campaigns and received decorations and medals when neither was present as a unit. Each of these situations is worthy of in depth study because invariably the circumstances which brought the individual or individuals to that particular place at that particular time is intriguing to say the least.

Regimental Music

by Warrant Officer Class One R Wearne, ARCM, psm
Bandmaster

Military music is as old as the Regiment itself for in the 1680s the authorisation granted to both Richard Leveson and the Scottish antecedents of Richard Cunningham instructed them to raise their troops by "beat of drums or otherwise". A Royal Warrant of 1684 had ordered that whilst dragoons should be classed as foot in garrison, when they took to the field they should be regarded as horse, and so although the transition of dragoons from being infantry with horses to being part of the cavalry proper had begun, they still manoeuvred to the beat of the drum. The noble trumpet at this stage, and until the middle of the next century, remained the prerogative of that superior arm, the regiments of Horse.

In the beginning, each troop was established for "... three score soldiers, one quartermaster, two sergeants, three corporals, two drummers and two hautboys (oboe players), besides Commissioned Officers". The drummer of dragoons was the counterpart of the trumpeter of Horse and, although mounted as the rest of his troop, he was not a kettle-drummer in these early days. He beat upon a single, large, infantry pattern, brass side drum which was slung from his right shoulder and rested upon his left thigh. The hautboy was not common in the army and, whilst familiar enough in civilian circles, its establishment in the military was exclusive to the dragoons and the Horse Grenadier Guards. His instrument was a primitive form of oboe of which the coarse double reed must have emitted a very piercing nasal bray. We know that the drummers beat the routine and executive calls in the field and in quarters, but the early duties of the hautboys are less clear. It is for conjecture, too, that the noise these fellows made gave rise to the unforgettable nickname bestowed upon the mounted branch by lesser mortals: The Donkey Wallopers! In any case, we can now see that with four musicians of a sort in each troop, a regiment of four or six troops had the potential to muster a band of 16 or 24 strong, and it is quite likely that the hautboys may have sounded their own version of certain routine calls such as "Reveille" and "Tattoo".

In 1765 all dragoon regiments were ordered to replace their drummers with trumpeters. The training of these trumpeters was clearly a matter of great importance for, in 1766, each regiment of dragoons was ordered to send two of its erstwhile drummers to Horse Guards "to be perfected in their Regimental Duties as Trumpeters". It was not until Christmas Day 1778 that George III granted an additional man and horse to the establishment of the King's Own Dragoons "as in ... other regiments having kettle-drums". The trumpeter of dragoons in the 1760s also had to carry and sound the bugle or "bugle-horn" as it was called then. Whilst the E flat cavalry trumpet, much as we know it today, was used for routine calls in quarters and for salutes, the B flat bugle which is not only easier to handle but also much easier to sound surely and, being of higher pitch, has a note which "carries" further, was used for executive calls in the field – changes of pace, formation and direction. The eight regimental trumpeters were expected to be versatile musicians for, when dismounted, they were to "form a band of musick, consisting of two French horns, two clarinettes and two bassoons...". The hautboys have disappeared without trace: there is no further mention of them and the assimilation of dragoons to the Horse was now complete.

The first official manual which laid down the notation of the regulation trumpet and bugle calls for the cavalry appeared in 1798, having been compiled by James Hyde, Trumpet-Major of the London and Westminster Light Horse. He did not compose the calls but was merely employed to collate them and regularise their notation. Their origin is obscure but, as most of Hyde's notation has survived virtually unchanged to reappear in the current manual *Trumpet and Bugle Calls for the Army* (HMSO 1966), it is reasonable to assume that the two former drummers who were sent up to Horse Guards by both Regiments, actually made Whitehall echo to the same notes of "Reveille", "Stables", "Boot and Saddle" and the other venerable cavalry calls that have summoned succeeding generations of Hussars all over the globe as those which are sounded in the regiment today.

Traditionally, whilst the infantry has always marched past to a quick-step (whether or not it also marched past in slow-time as well), the regiments of the cavalry very early on adopted a slow march which would be more fitting to their dignity and order of precedence in the Army List. These slow marches were not the funeral dirges like those to which dismounted troops would follow the coffin of some fallen comrade, but rather more the grand tunes of a triumphal or operatic entry. They were always played in "common" time and, apart from being ideal for walking past when mounted, they were well suited to marching past on foot at a pace somewhat slower than the regulation which would lead to a more exaggerated style of the men's bearing. They nearly all have a characteristic "pom, pom, pu-pom" ending to each section which lends itself to emphasis by the kettle-drums and has become a distinctive feature.

Unfortunately these cavalry marches were not authorised until 1903 and so, at this distance in time, it is difficult to determine when the tunes which interest us in particular were originally adopted. It would appear that General Bland's daughter was something of a composer and, in 1745, she wrote a piece which is variously known as "The Dettingen March", "General Bland's Inspection March" and the "Slow March of the 3rd Hussars". It is said that she wrote it to commemorate the "magnificent part" played by the King's Own Dragoons at Dettingen when General Bland was Colonel. The manuscript was discovered in Dublin Museum in 1920 and lent to the bandmaster of the time, A Hatherley. He arranged it as a regimental march and it was authorised as such until the amalgamation. In about 1789 General John Reid (who certainly held a commission in the Black Watch at some time and had, among other things, been Colonel of the Connaught Rangers) composed an air known as "The Garb of Auld Gaul". I cannot say when the 7th Hussars adopted it as the regimental slow march but, in common with several other regiments of Scottish origin, it was authorised as such in 1903.

As well as marching past at the Walk cavalry regiments would also march past at the Trot and, very occasionally, at the Canter, although this was known as a Gallop. Most regiments found "The Keel Row" their favourite for the Trot, whilst others habitually used "John Peel". These tunes were never authorised, but we do know that the 7th Hussars habitually used another favourite which was a Scottish air, "Monymusk". However, in 1898, whilst at Aldershot, it was found that because so many other mounted units in the garrison trotted past to "Monymusk", a degree of originality was called for and a popular dance tune of the day was adopted called "Encore". Nobody can tell, now, who the composer was, but the tune was very popular in late-Victorian and Edwardian ballrooms being used as an encore to the quadrille or lancers and hence, presumably, its name. The only other regiment to share it was the 9th Lancers.

Both Regiments used Scottish classics for the Gallop or Canter, and both tunes were extremely popular with other regiments as well. The 3rd Hussars used the most popular, "The Bonnets O' Bonnie Dundee", whilst the 7th Hussars favoured the tune which appears to have been second in the cavalry "charts", "The Campbells are Coming".

Strangely enough both Regiments enjoyed peculiar infantry-style quick marches which were unauthorised but, presumably, used for such occasions as church parades when they would be both dismounted and obliged to step out in time with other units at the regulation pace. For this purpose the 3rd Hussars used a march called "Robert the Devil" arranged by L Kappey from the final section of Meyerbeer's overture "Robert le Diable" composed in 1831. The 7th Hussars, uncharacteristically, for all its other music is of Scottish origin, used a march based on a traditional Leinster jig called "Brian O'Lynn's Breeches", although the Regiment called the march, "The Bannocks of Barley Meal" whilst the Gloucestershire Regiment, which also uses the same arrangement calls it, "The Kynegad Slashers".

Upon amalgamation, Bandmaster (now Major Retd) E G Horabin arranged an entirely new quick march of The Queen's Own Hussars on themes taken from Franz Von Suppé's overture "Light Cavalry". It has been said that these dashing, romantic themes, when reduced to the pace of a military quick march, have developed a certain grinding quality but the tune is unmistakable, it is unforgettable and, unlike the situation in several other regiments, there is not a soldier in The Queen's Own Hussars who does not know his regimental march. The authorised slow march of The Queen's Own Hussars is now a combination of the "3rd Hussars Slow March" and "The Garb of Auld Gaul".

Before closing this section, mention must be made of two other musical features which are peculiar to The Queen's Own Hussars. When the officers dine in mess together and the band plays the National Anthem after the port has been served, it is always preceded by the first eight bars of "God Save The Prince of Wales" which then runs straight into "God Bless The Queen" without pause. This was a custom of the 3rd Hussars but history does not relate how it arose.

Finally, when the Guidon is taken into church during a parade service and handed over to the chaplain for safe-keeping for the duration, it is the custom that its escort party brings it in at the slow march whilst the band plays the Regiment's slow march. Once the chaplain has the Guidon the escorts march away in quick time without music. Conversely, at the end of the service, the escorts approach the chaplain in quick time (usually during the final hymn). When the chaplain has returned the Guidon and given his blessing, the escort party marches out of church in slow time whilst the band plays "Fantasy" again.

"It is frequently the Custom amongst some of the Men when they see an Officer at a Distance to Sculk into a House before he comes up – by a standing rule in every Rigiment In the Army this practice is pointedly Forbid – It is mean and spiritless and gives every reason to Suppose they were so unsoulder like in their Dress and appearance that they were ashamed to be seen – any one guilty of it for the future may Depend on being Punished for It If this is not punctually complid with for wich the Non Commission Officers shall be responsible – there will be an order for regular Evening parade."

7TH HUSSARS' DAILY ORDERS HADDINGTON 24 JULY 1780

The Drum Horse Ensemble

by Major J E R Bulkeley Second-in-Command

Most mounted bands included a drumhorse and kettledrummer until their disbandment with mechanisation in the 1930s. However, to the Regiment, the drumhorse and the drums carried have been of special significance since 1743 and have survived mechanisation.

The original drums were one of four pairs captured from the French during the Battle of Dettingen in 1743. Unfortunately those drums were destroyed by fire while stored in the Tower of London in 1855. The existing drums, bought in 1856 by the officers as replacements, were made by Messrs Distin of London in solid silver. The most striking feature, musically, of these unique instruments is that they can be tuned in seven different keys by simply turning one screw. During the period 1834–1958 the 3rd Hussars carried their battle honours on the drums and shabraque. Thus the drums in effect replaced the Guidon and were held in the same esteem.

In 1766 all drummers became trumpeters, thus providing a trumpeter for each Troop in the Regiment. This was to cause "great inconvenience" for the 3rd Hussars, because if, as they wished, one kettledrummer was to remain employed with the drums, one Troop had no trumpeter. It was not until 1778 that the Colonel of the Regiment, Lieutenant-General Charles Fitzroy, gained permission from the Secretary of State for War, Viscount Barrington for the additional man and horse to be added to the establishment. This privilege was reaffirmed in 1959.

Early records show that the kettledrummer was a rank equivalent to sergeant and that various bandsmen over the years rode the drumhorse dressed and paid as kettledrummer sergeant regardless of their actual rank. In more modern times, it has been found easier to teach a groom to play the drums than a drummer to ride! As a result the Stables Troop have for the most part provided the kettledrummer, who to this day wears the silver collar presented to the Regiment by the wife of Charles Fitzroy, later Lord Southampton, on his appointment to command the Regiment in 1772.

Over the years many drumhorses have travelled the world with the Regiment; between 1927 and 1932 Mary served in Egypt and India before returning to York. When the 3rd Hussars mechanised, she was bought by the Regiment to continue the tradition. Gauntlet was the first horse to carry the drums after the Second World War when he first paraded at Bielefeld in 1952 ridden by K D Edwards. Silver Cannon was an outstanding tournament horse before carrying drums on the 1959 Guidon Parade. Crusader was presented to the Regiment by HRH The Princess Margaret, the last Colonel-in-Chief of the 3rd Hussars, in 1958, and he was succeeded in 1975 by the present drumhorse Dettingen who was presented to the Regiment by the Colonel-in-Chief, Her Majesty Queen Elizabeth the Queen Mother.

Sport

by Major T V Myatt, "A" Squadron Leader

Regimental sport and sporting achievements are sadly rarely mentioned in the early records of our founder regiments. This is, no doubt, mainly due to their involvement in numerous campaigns and internal security duties. It would appear that during the intervening periods of peace the Regiments were kept fully occupied with the then daily routine of cavalry. It may be of interest to note however, that in 1836, some 150 years after The Queen Consort's Regiment of Dragoons had been raised, due to the prevalence of crime and drunkenness within the British Army, the Royal Commission on Military Punishments recommended that soldiers should be urged to play "manly games". Racquets, fives, football and cricket were specially mentioned. Officers were not tarred with the same brush and pursued interests of hunting, racing on the flat, steeplechasing, shooting and fishing. The earliest success of note recorded was in 1851 when the Grand Military Steeplechase at Warwick was won by Fugleman, which was owned by Colonel Shirley and ridden by Lieutenant Frazer. In 1878, Chilblain, owned by Captain Paget won the same prized trophy at Sandown.

Polo, that most exciting of sports with natural appeal for the cavalry, was reintroduced in India in 1867, with the first inter-regimental game played at Hounslow Heath in 1871. The 7th Hussars who returned from India that year, were soon to become established as a fine polo-playing regiment. They won the Inter-Regimental Tournament for four consecutive years from 1883 until their return to India. Field-Marshal Earl Haig, KCB, KCIE, KCVO, then a young lieutenant, played in the team for two successful years. The Regiment maintained its success in India, twice winning the Inter-Regimental Tournament and playing in the final on three other occasions as well as winning numerous other tournaments – all in the space of nine years.

During the period before the Great War both Regiments continued to play polo and a few other sporting successes are worthy of mention. The 3rd Hussars won the Pretoria Cricket League, the first success of its kind to be recorded by either Regiment. Lieutenant Grubb 3rd King's Own Hussars won the Great Irish Horse Show in 1911 and in the same year Lieutenant McCalmont, who later became Colonel of the 7th Hussars, won the Grand Military Steeplechase on his own horse Vinegar Hill. Lieutenant McCalmont was the owner of The Tetrarch who was never beaten, and in 1913 as a two year old won seven races over five and six furlong courses with total winnings of £11,336, more than enough to pay the stable bill.

Between the World Wars both Regiments were to have their successes as well as the enjoyment of playing sport. The 3rd Hussars served in no less than five different countries during this period, experiencing, no doubt, the inevitable disruption associated with regimental moves. They won the Inter-Regimental at Ranelagh in 1920, in Egypt they won the Command Water Polo

League and in India they were their Brigade Hockey Champions as well as winners of the East India Railway boxing tournament. As if this was not proof of their sporting prowess, in 1922 the Regiment whilst in Constantinople had held a regimental sports event which was watched by a thousand spectators. On their return to England they missed winning the Regimental Jumping Team Cup at the Royal Tournament by half a point. The following year, 1936, they won the cup which was presented to them by Captain The Lord Strathcona and Mount Royal, who himself had been a 3rd Hussar. The 7th Hussars, apart from three years service in India, in which they won the All India Hockey Challenge Cup, were based in Britain. They had great success winning, to name but a few, the Scottish Command Hockey Championships in 1924, and the Command Football Cup in 1925, also reaching the Cavalry Cup final that year. In 1927 the Regiment excelled winning the Cavalry Cup, the Southern Command Boxing Championships, the Garrison Cricket Cup, the Aldershot Open Tournament and the Tidworth Junior Cup, as well as being finalists in the Subalterns Cup at polo. The same year Lieutenant Grosvenor won the Cheltenham Gold Cup and along with Lieutenant Thomas rode in the Grand National. A fellow officer, Lieutenant Talbot-Ponsonby, made regimental history by winning the King George V Gold Cup in 1930 at the International Horse Show. The following year he represented England at show-jumping in Canada and the United States, winning two prestige competitions. His success continued. In 1932 he won the Prince of Wales Cup at the International Horse Show, an achievement repeated in 1934 along with the World Open Championship at Aldershot. Most of Lieutenant Talbot-Ponsonby's successes were on Chelsea, a 7th Hussar troop-horse. (He later was to train the first ever victorious British Olympic show-jumping team.) In 1934 the Regiment again won the coveted Inter-Regimental Tournament and the following year the first regimental rugby team reached the finals of the Army Cup in Egypt, a trophy they won four years later. Both Regiments lost their horses on mechanisation in 1936 resulting in a greater emphasis on "dismounted" sports subsequently.

After the Second World War the 3rd Hussars were serving in Palestine and Syria where they became water-polo champions before moving to Germany. In 1948 Lieutenant-Colonel Sir Peter Farquhar, DSO, obtained nine couple of hounds from six of the most famous packs in England to give the Regiment its very own hunt from which a lot of sport was had; probably just as well due to the lack of sports fields at the time. In 1949, the Regiment won the Regimental Cross Country Team BAOR Championships, and again in 1952 with the Army Championships. Despite having been mechanised, cavalry traditions persisted and, from 1951, the Regiment won the BAOR Inter-Regimental Polo Tournament for three successive years and provided three team members for the BAOR show-jumping team, one of whom Lieutenant Dallas also represented Great Britain. Also in 1951, the Regiment won the 1 (BR) Corps Inter-Unit Cup for ski-ing. In the period coming up to amalgamation, the 3rd Hussars were to maintain their presence at cross country running and ski-ing and make in-roads at basketball, sailing and table tennis.

The 7th Hussars had also initially had problems with sports fields after the Second World War as well as demobilisation. However, by 1952 the Regiment had moved to Germany and were divisional champions at cross country running, novice boxing and hockey. That year they had a successful racing season winning 10 races and sharing "leading stable" with the 9th Lancers. The move out to the Far East was not to disrupt the racing success, finishing second on the winners list in Hong Kong despite only having been present for half the season. Other successes included the Army Hockey League, Football Cup, rugby, swimming and basketball. On its return to England the Regiment, prior to amalgamation in 1958, won the Cavalry Cup and the Inter-Regimental Polo Tournament.

Following amalgamation The Queen's Own Hussars continued the sporting successes of their forebears. From 1963 for five consecutive years they won the United Services Challenge Cup at polo, having won either the UK or BAOR Inter-Regimental Tournament beforehand. In 1973 the UK Inter-Regimental was again won and in 1982 we reached the finals.

The regimental football team have regularly featured in their divisional leagues with wins in 1961 and 1977. The Cavalry Cup is as important today as it ever has been, and the level of success is worthy of note, with six appearances in the finals of which the Regiment was victorious on two occasions. In addition in 1974 the Regiment won both the South-West District League and Cup. The Regiment has had both strong football and hockey teams. The hockey team won the BAOR Cup in 1964 as well as being finalists in the Army Cup in the same year. The Jubilee Cup which has been keenly competed for, since 1970, by RAC regiments has to date been won three times with two other appearances in the finals. The Regiment has often been well placed in the Divisional League not least in 1983 as winners.

Skiing has become a major source of success for the Regiment. Annually a merry band of men have deserted the tank park by late November, much to the chagrin of the rest of the Regiment, rarely to return before Easter bearing trophies to appease their envious colleagues. Victories at divisional level are too numerous to mention. Since 1974 we have been UKLF Alpine Team Champions three times, BAOR Alpine Team Champions twice and in 1982 and 1983 overall Army Champions. Captains Kemmis-Betty and James, Lance-Corporal Dryden and Lieutenant MacInnes all skied for the army team with Lieutenant MacInnes twice being the Inter-Services Champion.

It has not been possible to give mention of every sport and the related successes in this short article. Sport has, however, played a significant part in regimental life when the opportunities have existed. Perhaps most important of all is the enjoyment it has provided for so many members of the Regiment as well as a share of success.

The First Regimental Polo Team
The 3rd Hussars played the 16th Lancers in Bombay 1873

Armoured car patrol in Haifa. 3rd Hussars. 1948

Armoured car patrol in Aden. The Queen's Own Hussars. 1967

Musical ride. 3rd Hussars. Aldershot 1920
Inspected by His Majesty King George V on 22 May

A 300 Year Party

by Major M J Parker, MBE
Regular Army Reserve of Officers

I feel quite certain that the day after "The Queen Consort's Regiment of Dragoons" was formed in 1685 someone said – "Let's have a party, the commissariat will do all the work and we'll get a wagon of birds from London." This ancient tradition has been continued to this day and the time and effort which has gone into these celebrations has only on few occasions been eclipsed by the more serious activity of being professional killers.

I took over after 276 years to find that very few of the original files still existed so we started from scratch. Scratch being basically – "Blackie" – our demon quartermaster who revelled in achieving the impossible. Someone said that it was easier to get a 700 by 70 feet Taj Mahal built than it was to write-off a gasmask, but I am sure that this is not true.

I have always worked to three basic rules: 1. If it is easy to do it's not worth doing. 2. If you know it is going to work you are probably doing the wrong thing. 3. Unless everybody enjoys it – don't bother.

We started with the Taj Mahal, painted by one Trooper Child who was 6 ft 10 ins and could not fit into a Centurion, and progressed to "Moscow". I have now burnt Moscow more times than Napoleon could ever have imagined but that first time took some beating. At the end of the long lawn at Detmold a great structure – the band playing in the bushes – 'volunteers' in full dress being blown up behind the guns – fireworks and finally the whole thing going up in a sheet of flames. Moscow was some 20 yards in front of Colonel Pat Howard-Dobson's house and I was impressed with his coolness as the trees caught fire. Destined for higher things I thought.

We went to Berlin next and the odd little show in front of 100,000 seemed to go quite well so I tried Moscow again. The Foreign Office decreed that it had to burn quickly so we had fire-engines spraying the structure with kerosene and when the moment came it went up with an enormous explosion and a sheet of flame 200 feet high and the 800 musicians stopped playing to watch – no-one seemed to notice except the conductor.

Brussels, Wembley, Lulworth – another Moscow but this time with all the napalm left over from the *Torrey Canyon* and fifty Chieftain HESH rounds going off at once, and Vesuvius and Pompeii – with prisoners pumping kerosene up to the top of the volcano to keep it going. Sadly they were a little too enthusiastic at the rehearsal in the afternoon and everything burnt down. I tried to explain to drunken guests that evening that this was Pompeii after the defence cuts, ie no eruption.

On to Hohne and my regimental swan-song. I am not certain why we chose to recreate the Battle of Trafalgar in a cavalry mess a few hundred miles inland but it seemed a good idea at the time. Assault boats were made up into Men of War, the band floated in the middle of the lake. The boats appeared propelled by clerks in frogmens suits (I was adjutant at the time) pressing buttons to let off the broadsides – sadly one went into the band by mistake, but did not seem to affect the sound of the music. Rather before the cue the boats caught fire as did the trees and a number of other things. The aluminium boats melted and sank – the band continued to play although lost in the smoke and frogmen appeared amongst the mess kits complaining that the water was F****G HOT and General Jackie Harman turned to Colonel Mike Pritchard and said "I have a horrible feeling that I am the Senior Officer present." The Court of Inquiry was hilarious.

So I left to do lesser things. The Royal Tournament, Aldershot Army Display, The Silver Jubilee, The Royal Fireworks and the largest Childrens Party in history (180,000 screaming brats) not to mention Son et Lumieres and world wide extravaganzas have all seemed just a training for when the geriatrics are asked back to have a go again. In the meantime "Nec aspera terrent".

Editor's Note. I sympathise with Major Parker: some of the 300 year old files have, unaccountably, got lost – but not all the records. The illustration facing page 73 demonstrates that Tattoos were thriving during the 1920s. And accounts survive. To many of the immediate post-war generation of troop leaders, Colonel Francis Jayne was an awe-inpiring, if not terrifying, figure. It cannot always have been thus, for shortly after joining the Regiment in 1925 he was selected to play the maiden in the re-enactment of St George and the Dragon at the famous Tidworth Tattoo. The Dragon was a large and magnificent beast, built by the local workshops, with flashing eyes, tossing head and tongues of flame belching from its mouth. It had only one drawback: it was heavily dependent on electricity. The first three performances went without a hitch, St George arriving just in time to slay the Dragon and save the maiden. On the final night, in front of a most august and distinguished audience, the Dragon came on exactly on cue and St George was heard in the distance galloping to the rescue. At this moment, however, the Dragon shuddered to a halt, his head and neck collapsed, his eyes dimmed to black and the flames disappeared. In the still and now darkened arena from the Dragon's mouth issued for all to hear the immortal words, "F . . . it. The f . . . . . . battery's f . . . . ." The maiden's blushes were covered by the night. I am told, however, that to this day St George has not recovered from his fall.

The Fairer Sex

by Mrs David Jenkins
Wife of The Commanding Officer

If army wives of today sometimes feel aggrieved about the condition of quarters or the upheaval of military life in general, it is evident that their plight has improved out of all possible recognition in the last century or so. Until the late 19th century only six or seven per cent of other ranks were allowed to marry, although probably at least another seven per cent were married without leave. There was no legal ban to marriage, but only those wives officially sanctioned, whose names appeared on the Married Roll, were provided for by the state. Any others were totally unrecognised. Not that life for "official" wives was easy: there were no married quarters built before 1852, and prior to that most wives lived with their husbands and children in barrack rooms with single soldiers, often separated only by a hanging blanket. Children were born and brought up in these over-crowded, ill-heated and ill-ventilated rooms. The number of married soldiers was so severely restricted because of "the inconvenience of having a large train attached to a regiment, and of the expense of moving that train from station to station". Nevertheless, it seems that in the 1850s there was a floating population of about 10,000 women and children in the army, other than enlisted boys.

When regiments were sent abroad, only a limited number of the women married with leave were allowed to accompany their husbands. They drew lots for the places, while those left behind were given money to go to any part of the United Kingdom they chose, after which they were given no further assistance. If any wife who did accompany her husband was widowed, she lost her allowance and therefore her livelihood, unless she remarried within six months. Some wives of the 3rd Light Dragoons had had three or four husbands by the end of the first Sikh War.

At the other end of the scale, husbands could make life difficult for wives left behind on foreign campaigns. Lieutenant-Colonel Vivian, Commanding the 7th Hussars in the Peninsular campaign in 1813, wrote a series of letters to his wife, entreating her to send him everything from ham, tongue, butter, cheese and wine to six couple of hounds, to a detailed list of further items of clothing necessary if the campaign should continue. Later his wife received a sharp reprimand for failing to inform her husband of the name of the man or the ship to which she had entrusted these articles: "Oh, Eliza, after having been married to me for nine years and a half, to be so *very* thick!"

For sheer arrogance however, it is difficult to cap the remark made by the 6th Duke of Somerset to his second wife when she dared touch him with her fan: "Madam, my first Duchess was a Percy, and *she* never took such a liberty!" He also denied his daughter £20,000 of her inheritance "for having sat down in his presence".

Despite all the very real difficulties and hardships suffered by many wives in the 18th and 19th centuries some showed a remarkable degree of courage and adventurism. One such was Mary Ralphson, wife of Trooper Ralph Ralphson of the King's Own Dragoons, who sailed with the regiment in 1742, and at the age of 45 fought with her husband at the Battle of Dettingen. When one of the dragoons "fell wounded by her side", she "equipped herself" in his "uniform and accoutrements ... mounted his charger and regained the battle-line". She was with her husband at several such engagements, including the Battle of Fontenoy. Evidently this life agreed with her for she lived until the grand age of 110, dying in 1808 in Liverpool.

Aristocrat's wives also had their share of adventure, as the daughter of the Marquess of Anglesey who, when attending a review of the 7th Queen's Own Hussars in 1819 with her father, was observed to be minus her right hand which she had lost while attending her husband at one of the battles in Spain.

In 1692 the 7th Hussars were ordered to Edinburgh to disperse a mob of women agitating on behalf of the Edinburgh Garrison for arrears of pay — "a multitude of women comes here to infest and threaten Major General Mackay". Sadly, there is no record of how the task was accomplished.

"Marriage is to be discouraged as much as possible. Officers must explain to the men the many miseries that women are exposed to, and by every sort of persuasion they must prevent their marrying if possible."

RULES AND REGULATIONS FOR CAVALRY 1795

CHAPTER SIX

Affiliations

The Sherbrooke Hussars

The Sherbrooke Hussars trace their origins back to 21 September 1866 when the Sherbrooke Battalion of Infantry was formed from six independent rifle companies. The first commanding officer was Lieutenant-Colonel the Right Honourable Lord Aylmer, a former Governor-General of Canada. In 1900 this battalion split into three regiments. Although none of these regiments were mobilised as units during the 1914–1918 war, many of the men volunteered for the Canadian Expeditionary Force and fought in France.

In the 1936 amalgamation the three regiments were reduced to two, becoming The Sherbrooke Regiment (MG) and the 7th/11th Hussars. During the 1939–1945 war The Sherbrooke Regiment amalgamated with Les Fusiliers de Sherbrooke to become the 27th Armoured Regiment. They landed with 2nd Canadian Armoured Brigade in Normandy and fought in the North-West Europe Campaign until VE Day. Only one tank survived from "D" to "VE" Day. Meanwhile the 7th/11th Hussars mobilised as Headquarters Squadron, 2nd Canadian Armoured Brigade, but also provided 16 officers and 383 men for The Royal Rifles of Canada in Newfoundland and Hong Kong.

In 1965 The Sherbrooke Regiment RCAC and the 7th/11th Hussars RCAC amalgamated to form The Sherbrooke Hussars, an armoured regiment equipped with the Cougar AFV.

3rd/9th South Australian Mounted Rifles

In 1839 South Australia was the first of the three Australian colonies to raise its own military force: the Adelaide Lancers. However, after a few months a state financial crisis led to the regiment's demise. Nevertheless, when the Adelaide Mounted Rifle Corps was formed in 1854, a number of the original volunteers rejoined. All ranks were expected to provide their own horses and arms for which they received no pay.

During the Boer War the equivalent of a squadron saw service with the Bushmen's Contingent. In their first action three troopers were awarded DCMs. In the 1914–1918 war the unit was expanded to form the 3rd and 9th Light Horse Regiments, both of whom distinguished themselves at Gallipoli and in Palestine, the 9th being the only regiment to capture a Turkish regiment's battle standard. In the 1939–1945 war, the 2nd/9th Armoured Regiment, the successor to the 9th Light Horse, equipped with Matilda and Grant tanks, took part in the bitter fighting to clear the islands to the north of Australia.

Soon after 1945 the two regiments were amalgamated and given their present title. In 1975 the regiment was reduced in strength to an independent squadron equipped with the American M113 family of vehicles with which to carry out its role of medium reconnaissance.

Queen Alexandra's (Waikato/Wellington East Coast) Squadron Royal New Zealand Armoured Corps

Queen Alexandra's (Waikato/Wellington East Coast) Squadron has been based on three separate North Island units which have a long history of amalgamation. They are 2nd Queen Alexandra's Mounted Rifles, 4th Waikato Mounted Rifles, and 9th Wellington East Coast Mounted Rifles.

After the Land Wars and the subsequent withdrawal of colonial forces, most volunteer cavalry units were either disbanded or declined. However, volunteers were still active enough to form the basis of a major contribution by the three regiments in the Boer War, for which they earned a battle honour. They fought again with distinction during the 1914–1918 war in the New Zealand Mounted Rifles Brigade at Gallipoli and in Egypt and the Sinai. In 1942 the regiments were mechanised and many individuals from them fought in the Middle East.

Many reorganisations followed in the period 1945–1982, but the squadron is now part of the Territorial Force, equipped for a reconnaissance role with CVR(T) Scorpion and the M113 A1.

4th Worcestershire Cadet Squadron Army Cadet Force

by Major B J Somner
Squadron Leader

The Army Cadet Force traces its origins back to the 1860s when, fearing a French invasion, the Counties raised volunteer battalions. In many cases boys' companies were raised as adjuncts to these battalions. As the invasion threat diminished, so the social benefits of these companies became recognised, and from then the Army Cadet Force has had a continuous existence, sometimes, as now, with strong official backing, sometimes having to rely almost exclusively on private efforts.

The basic unit of the Army Cadet Force is the detachment of one officer, two adult instructors, and about 30 cadets. In 1950 the 4th Battalion of the Worcestershire Army Cadet Force was formed, affiliated mainly to the Yeomanry. In 1959 the battalion changed its title to the present one on becoming affiliated to The Queen's Own Hussars. Squadron Headquarters and one Troop are based at Bromsgrove, with other Troops at Droitwich, Redditch, Winyates and Rubery.

"A" Squadron (Warwickshire and Worcestershire Yeomanry) The Queen's Own Mercian Yeomanry

The history of "A" Squadron, The Queen's Own Mercian Yeomanry began in 1794 with the formation of The Warwickshire Yeomanry in July and the Worcester Yeomanry Cavalry in September of that year. Both Regiments were raised as a counter to the ambitions of Napoleon and had two main roles: the defence of the United Kingdom and the suppression of riots and public disorders. Indeed in this latter role both Regiments saw action at different times in Birmingham and Worcester.

During the Boer War, Yeomanry Regiments were invited to serve abroad for the first time and the Warwickshire Yeomanry despatched a full squadron as well as sponsoring five Imperial Yeomanry companies. The Queen's Own Worcester Hussars, as they were now titled, sponsored two such companies and sustained more casualties than any other regiment of Imperial Yeomanry in that campaign.

Both Regiments played a full part in the First World War, seeing action at Gallipoli, in Palestine and the Canal Zone. The Warwickshire Yeomanry took part in the famous charge at Huj in 1917, covering a distance of 1500 yards during which 12 Turkish guns were captured and their crews sabred at their posts. By coincidence, two squadrons of The Worcester Hussars also participated in this charge.

After the end of the war The Worcester Hussars were converted to gunners. During the Second World War they went to France in 1940 with the BEF fighting a successful rearguard action before being evacuated at Dunkirk. Subsequently, they saw action as a field artillery regiment during the invasion of France in June 1944. In 1947, the Worcestershire Yeomanry was re-created as an anti-tank regiment but in 1950 became a regiment of the Royal Armoured Corps, affiliated to the 7th Queen's Own Hussars.

The Warwickshire Yeomanry moved with their horses to Palestine in 1939, and remained part of 4th Cavalry Brigade until they converted to tanks in 1941 and became part of the 8th Army. They fought with great gallantry at El Alamein, alongside the 3rd Hussars, where they smashed through an enemy gun line, whilst themselves losing 53 out of their 60 tanks. After re-equipping they later served with distinction in the Italian campaign until the end of the war.

In 1956 the two Regiments amalgamated becoming The Queen's Own Warwickshire and Worcestershire Yeomanry, but thirteen years later, following defence cuts, the Regiment was reduced to a cadre. It was from this cadre that in 1971 "A" (Warwickshire and Worcestershire) Squadron of the Queen's Own Mercian Yeomanry was formed. Initially, the Regiment had an infantry role in Home Defence. However, on 1 April 1983, following an expansion of the TA, this role was changed to one of Home Defence reconnaissance.

Thus nearly 200 years later – and after many changes in organisation and equipment – the Regiment reverted to a role very similar to the one its ancestors had back in 1794 – except that it is now mounted in Land Rovers instead of on horses! Today "A" Squadron is based at Stourbridge and Coventry and still retains strong links with The Queen's Own Hussars, who provide the permanent staff instructors for the Squadron.

HMS *Birmingham*

The first HMS *Birmingham*, a light cruiser of 5440 tons, was commissioned in 1914. Early in the First World War she rammed and sank the German submarine U15, the first ever recorded action of this kind. She was in action at Heligoland Bight, Dogger Bank, and Jutland, for all three of which she earned battle honours.

The second HMS *Birmingham*, a heavy cruiser of 9000 tons, won a battle honour off Norway in 1940 close to where a Troop of the 3rd Hussars was at sea. She later sailed with the convoys relieving Malta and was torpedoed and badly damaged. However, she was able, after repair, to resume convoy duties and earned another battle honour off Korea in 1952–1953.

The third, and current HMS *Birmingham*, was commissioned in 1976, the second Type 42 Destroyer of the *Sheffield* class. She displaces 4500 tons. This year she undergoes her main half-life refit. Since 1980 our links with HMS *Birmingham* have grown, based on our mutual connections with the City of Birmingham.

HMS *Naiad*

The first HMS *Naiad*, named after the mythical water nymph, was captured from the French in the West Indies in 1783. The second, a 38-gun frigate, was built at Limehouse in 1797. She greatly distinguished herself in many actions during the Napoleonic Wars and earned her first battle honour "Trafalgar 1805".

The third HMS *Naiad* was a twin-screw steel cruiser. She displaced 3400 tons and was launched at Barrow in 1890. The fourth, a Dido Class Cruiser, was commissioned in 1940 and her first main action, for which she was awarded the battle honour "Crete 1941", was in the same campaign in which "C" Squadron, 3rd Hussars fought. She later earned the further battle honours "Mediterranean 1941" and "Malta Convoys 1941–1942", but on 11 March 1942 she was torpedoed amidships by U565 and sank in 20 minutes with the loss of 2 officers and 80 men.

The present HMS *Naiad*, the eighth of the 2900 ton Leander Class Frigates, was commissioned in 1965. The links with the Regiment were established soon afterwards and since then there have been frequent exchange visits, including officers and soldiers from the Regiment cruising with her to Germany and the Caribbean.

2nd Polish Corps

For over a thousand years the Polish nation has been one of the main bulwarks of European Christendom against invasion from the east. In 1683 – two years before the raising of the Regiment – King Sobieski of Poland led an allied army to the relief of Vienna. The largest national contingent was 20,000 Polish cavalry, armed mostly with lances. After a forced march on their sturdy horses, they delivered the charge which routed the Turkish army in one of the decisive battles of the western world. Over one hundred years later, Napoleon, with a false promise of freedom for Poland, recruited regiments of Polish Lancers into his army. They proved formidable cavalry.

In 1939 Poland was overwhelmed when, fighting valiantly and single-handed against the Germans to their west, the Soviet Union attacked them from the east. In 1940 the Soviet Union murdered over 10,000 Polish officer prisoners of war whose bodies were found mostly in the Katyn Forest. However, after the Soviet Union was itself attacked by Germany, the remaining Poles in captivity were released. After many tribulations these came out through Iran to form the basis of the 2nd Polish Corps.

Joining the Eighth Army in Italy, the Corps was given the task of leading the final assault on the formidable Monte Cassino position. Shortly before the attack, General Anders, the Corps Commander, was told that Great Britain could no longer guarantee the freedom and integrity of Poland – the cause for which in 1939 Great Britain had declared war on Hitler's Germany – against the power of the Soviet Empire. In view of this, he was offered the opportunity to withdraw his Corps from further operations. This offer he rejected and the Corps captured Monte Cassino. They continued to fight until the end of the campaign in 1945, and many Poles lie buried in allied cemeteries in Italy.

Shortly before he died WO1 O'Connor told the story of the most remarkable example of chivalry that he had ever witnessed – and he was no mean judge, a soldier of great experience and the holder of the MM. On one occasion in Italy, when as SSM of "A" Squadron, he found himself commanding the rear link tank which was located near a Polish Field Dressing Station. Casualties were so heavy in this battle that the FDS could not cope with the numbers coming in. However, to Mr O'Connor's astonishment, whenever a 7th Hussar tank crewman was brought in he was taken, on the insistence of both staff and the Polish casualties, to the head of the queue. In wearing the 2nd Polish Corps sign of the Maid of Warsaw, we are linked to this chivalrous tradition.

Links with the City of Birmingham

Before 1958 cavalry regiments, unlike the infantry, had no permanent County links. However, these were established just after the 3rd and 7th Hussars had been amalgamated to form The Queen's Own Hussars. The Regiment was given the West Midlands, Warwickshire, and Worcestershire, from where it has recruited ever since.

Of course much of the equipment used over the centuries by the Regiment has been made in Birmingham or the surrounding areas, from swords to major components of armoured fighting vehicles. Still in the possession of the Regiment is a sword made by "Woolley and Co., Birm 1794" for the 7th Light Dragoons.

Every year, whenever possible, the Lord Mayor of Birmingham visits the Regiment and twice a year, once at home and once away, the Regiment plays a West Midland Police Team at football. On Remembrance Sunday a contingent of Old Comrades is always on parade in Birmingham.

In the Tercentenary Year the Regiment is greatly honoured in being granted the Freedom of the City.

CHAPTER SEVEN

Horse to Tank
Victorian Soldiering

by Lieutenant-Colonel D J M Jenkins
Commanding Officer

It is hard to discuss a subject as broad as Victorian soldiering in a single article – the period covers the time when officers purchased their commissions (Sir Hugh McCalmont bought a captaincy in the 7th Hussars for £5125 in 1869), and the time when Cardwell abolished the system and reorganised the army. However, the paragraphs below may well convince the soldier of the 1980s that his lot could be a great deal worse.

Soldier Recruiting. Recruiters were paid a bounty for recruits and so concentrated on likely locations – especially around pubs. Recruits were generally enlisted between the ages of 17/18 and 25. The social standing of the army was not high and the majority of recruits came from the lowest classes. During the 1870s a civilian employer stated, "men who spend too much of their money on drink, and waste their time in dissipation, frequently, as a last resort, go into the Army".

Living Accommodation. Soldiers lived and ate in barrack-rooms – these were large bare rooms with a stove, two tables and four benches and beds. Lockers were introduced during the period but the soldier used the room – and tables – for cleaning kit and for living. Windows were only opened with reluctance, and conditions of hygiene were not high. Pint basins were used for drinking, cleaning kit or making coffee as conditions demanded. A recruit was invariably given the worst bed space and the least amount of food, and expected to "lend" his seniors items of kit they had lost.

Riding School. Few recruits had ridden before, and their first requirement was to pass the riding school. No saddles were allowed initially, and no stirrups for a period after that.

Daily Routine. Once he had passed off, the recruit could expect the daily routine to be on the following lines:

    0630 reveille, wash, shave, lay out kit for inspection
    0700 first stables, muck out and exercise
    0800 breakfast
    0900 drill (on horseback)
    1045 grooming and kit cleaning
    1300 dinner
    1400 musketry practice

    1500 drill
    1630 tea
    1700 stables
    1800 stand down

Pay. In the 1870s a soldier earned 1s and 2d a day (about 6p). He got a pound of bread and $\frac{3}{4}$ pound of meat free each day, but had to buy butter, cheese, eggs, beer, coffee, and any other food he wanted. He paid stoppages for washing and hair cutting (1d a month), and for barrack damages. Little money was likely to be left over but the majority of that went on beer (at about 2d a pint). He could earn extra pay by becoming a specialist such as a rough rider or a gymnastic instructor, and he got 1d a day for each good conduct badge – given after each two year period of crime-free soldiering.

Punishment. Flogging in peacetime was abolished in 1868 and flogging in the field was abolished in 1881. Field punishment No 1 involved being lashed to a gun wheel and was awarded for serious offences in the field. Penal servitude was often awarded at courts martial, and regiments ran punishment drill parades for offenders who wore full kit weighing 40 or 50 pounds for the hour long periods. The guardroom for prisoners had a wooden board as a bed, with no blankets (unless sentenced to more than 7 days), and all those sent to the guardroom were given a very severe haircut.

India. Both 3rd Hussars and 7th Hussars served in India as part of the garrison of the country. Native labour considerably eased the tasks of the trooper as all cleaning and grooming tasks were done by Indians. However, the trooper had to contend with disease and boredom. The poor diet, drink and the climate caused a mass of disease problems – in the mid-1870s one quarter of 3rd Hussars were constantly on the sick list. Because all the onerous and time-consuming tasks were done for him, the trooper had little to fill his day. Men took to keeping pets or collecting butterflies or catching cobras.

The Suffolk Road Riot. Northern Ireland. August 1973

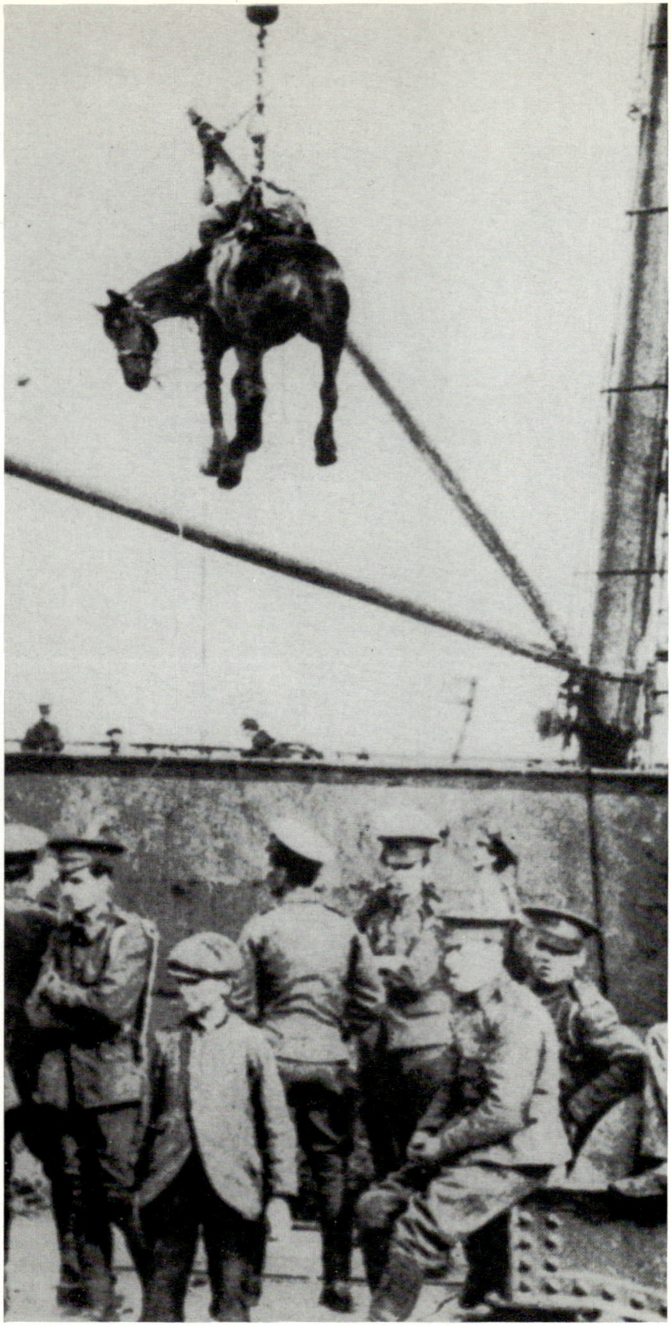

Loading tanks for Aden. "C" Squadron, The Queen's Own Hussars. Southampton. 1960

(*left*)
Unloading horses. 3rd Hussars. Boulogne. 1914

Field Service Marching Order No 1

Saddlery and Equipment in the 1930's

by Major J S Sutherland, MBE
Regimental Secretary 1962–1982

The saddle in use in the 1930's was the Universal Pattern 1912. It was rather cumbersome with a front iron arch called the pommel and a rear arch or cantel rising above the seat – a relic it may be assumed from the days of chivalry when knights in their ponderous armour needed a buttress in front and rear to keep them in position. The 1912 saddle was made to suit horses and cobs and gave one size for all Service purposes other than officers. The jointed front and rear arches were brought to the notice of officers of the British Army by General Keith Fraser, CMG, Inspector General of Cavalry, who had obtained one in Austria c.1887, where it had been invented by a small saddler. Both Sir Evelyn Wood and Veterinary Major Smith took a great interest in the saddle, and Sir Evelyn, agreed with Smith that "as far as the side bars and arches and this new attachment it is the acme of a soldier's saddle".

On the nearside in full marching order was the saddle wallet containing the trooper's small kit strapped to the front arch with a folded groundsheet/cape. On the nearside rear of the saddle a shoecase was attached which contained a spare pair of shoes to fit the horse (most troopers were trained in the art of cold shoeing in an emergency). A frog on the shoecase carried the sword and scabbard. Strapped to the scabbard was a mallet, picketing peg, hay net, shackle and rope, surcingle and pad, and a nose bag with one day's ration.

On the off-side went the rifle bucket which carried the .303 Lee Enfield rifle, the trooper's main armament when dismounted. On the rifle bucket was carried the mess tin and canvas water bucket.

The saddle was seated on a folded horse blanket, in full marching order a spare blanket was also carried on top of the horse blanket. The saddle was secured by the girth and surcingle. The bridle or headdress was made of leather, to which was fitted the universal pattern reversible or elbow bit, with curb chain. Secured to the bit were the reins, which ran back on each side of the neck to the rider's hands as he sits in the saddle. A white head rope was around the horse's neck attached to the headdress.

The average weight carried by the troop horse was 18 stone, but in 1934 this was reduced to 16 stone by the introduction of transport to carry the greatcoat and one day's ration instead of two.

Editor's Note. Major Sutherland joined the Cheshire Yeomanry in 1934 as a trooper. In 1941, as a troop sergeant, he took part in the last major horsed action of the British Army: against the Vichy French in Syria. After further service in The Derbyshire Yeomanry, he joined the 7th Hussars in 1950.

A Day in Barracks in the Life of a Trooper – 1935

by Major A S C Blackshaw, MBE
Quartermaster 1955–1970

In the 1930's the association with horses produced a type of individual who considered himself a cut above the foot sloggers, and could be found in all regiments where "stables" formed part of the daily routine.

Men enlisted in the Cavalry of the Line and were then posted to regiments. The 7th Hussars in the mid-'30s were stationed in Hounslow; living accommodation was above the stables, thus ensuring that troops were always available for the everlasting needs of the horse. With the closing down of the Cavalry Depot, Canterbury, recruits trained with their regiments. Training was hard and covered square bashing, riding school, and the ever present spit and polish.

The trained cavalryman was always fully occupied: every day horses had to be exercised, watered, fed, mucked out, groomed, plus saddlery and accoutrements cleaned and polished. Mounted parades, mounted skill at arms, manoeuvres were all part of his role, and his life was always bounded by the horse and its needs.

Food was good but basic (you only had one choice). There was the daily rush to meals to ensure a seat near the head of a table where two old sweats collected the food and dished it out.

Walking out was in uniform, unless you had a civilian clothes pass (after 18 months' service). Hounslow sported many pubs to the delight of the soldier who was invariably without money by midweek. However, if he was the proud possessor of one shilling, his evening night out was assured.

1 pint of beer	4 pence
10 fags	4 pence
1 hot pie	4 pence

The UK tour of the 7th Hussars was nearing its end and they duly left for Egypt by troopship in 1935. The voyage was uneventful except for the sleeping arrangements which were hammocks. These had to be taken down each morning and stowed away so that the space left could be used for messing and leisure.

Arrival in Egypt heralded a different way of life though the needs of the horse were the same. Training invariably finished at midday, leaving afternoons for outdoor sports and other activities. Social life was limited; there was a leave camp near Alexandria, and troops pursued hobbies in barracks. Walking out was in uniform and Cairo offered a night-life that was always an attraction.

In 1936 the last mounted parade took place and mechanisation overtook the 7th Hussars; it was completed by 1937. For the cavalryman and his horse it was the end of an era....

Mechanisation

It is almost impossible for those of us of later generations to imagine the trauma that mechanisation caused at the time. The cavalryman of the 1930s was fiercely proud that he was the inheritor of a tradition of excellence and chivalry stretching back to the medieval knight and legend. In spite of the mawkish excesses of some writers, he had a genuine affection for even the most refractory of his mounts. To this already charged atmosphere were added the bitter controversies between the advocates of the horse and the tank. As late as 1922 the 7th Hussar, Field-Marshal Earl Haig, with all the authority of the victorious commander-in-chief of the First World War, could say in a RUSI lecture "I am all for using aeroplanes and tanks, but they are only accessories to the man and the horse, and I feel sure that as time goes on you will find just as much use for the horse – the well-bred horse – as you have ever done in the past". It is easy to be critical now, but in those days the arguments must have appeared more nicely balanced.

In 1934 the Inspector of Cavalry had been asked "to select a cavalry regiment to carry out an experiment in mechanisation to replace horsed cavalry". This unwelcome honour fell to the 3rd Hussars, but, true to their traditions, they decided that "the only course was to give the experiment a real and whole hearted trial". During 1936 only "A" Squadron was converted – and then only to the 15 cwt box car. It was not until 1937 that the first troops of tanks arrived and even by the Munich crisis of September 1938 there were only enough to equip one squadron; the rest of the Regiment had to train with flags and trucks.

In 1927 the 7th Hussars were equipped with 14 six-wheelers to reduce the weight on the horse from 20 to 18 stone and to carry the eight Vickers machine-guns. Soon after this, two Austin Sevens were issued for reconnaissance. However, it was not until May 1936 in Egypt that the order to mechanise was given. Like the 3rd, the 7th Hussars decided to make the best of it. The other ranks were given the option of transferring to unmechanised regiments; it says much for the esprit de corps that only 16 out of 531 did so. The conversion was complete by January 1937.

As Major Blackshaw writes in another article "it was the end of an era". Life was centred round the horse: for 365 days a year he had to be watered, fed, mucked out, groomed and exercised; likewise in sport, from polo to tent pegging. So much has been lost; but the Regiment, free now to lock up its tanks in garages for days at a time, is able to take part in an even wider variety of adventurous sports. The horse has gone, except for recreation, but the spirit of the cavalryman lives on.

A Day in the Life of a Trooper – 1980

by Lance-Corporal Sword
A Serving Junior Non Commissioned Officer

At last they reach the new location, a troop hide. All engines are silenced. Inside the turret steam is rising off four freshly made cups of coffee laced with cherry brandy. Outside the rest of the crew are struggling with the camouflage nets and wooden poles. Guards and radio watches are organised as sleeping bags are rolled onto hot engine decks. Soon they contain weary bodies trying to snatch a few hours sleep. One of the bodies grumbles aloud, he drew the doomwatch stag!

Morning breaks to find them cocooned in their "green maggots" stirring as the guard awakens them. Drivers carry out first parade on their tanks. All the commanders disappear for a briefing. Breakfast is served, bacon and egg "Banjos", complete with oily fingerprints and a hot brew.

Movement orders are issued and all equipment quickly stowed. Everyone gets into position, headsets on. The radios are tuned and the gun is put onto stabiliser as they prepare for the oncoming mock battle. The driver accelerates away trying to avoid the worst bumps as each bad jolt will bring him a stream of abuse from the rest of the crew! The gunner traverses left and right scanning the ground in front. He spots a target and engages as the commander fires his GPMG and throws smoke grenades. Over the air excited voices make their contact reports. The infantry move in and it is nearly over, strip wood is soon taken.

In convoy now on a "candy striped" road moving towards a rolling replen. The vibrating tank makes it hard for the gunner to stay awake as he wonders if there will be a letter.

A kick from the commander disturbs his dreaming. Gunner and loader stand balanced on the engine decks ready to inject diesel into the tank. That completed, the gunner races up the line of the replen with a jerry can in hand. He collects the mail and rations then stands and waits to be collected as the squadron rolls by.

Halted in a squadron leaguer for a non-tactical phase, maintenance takes priority, then onto a truck for a refreshing shower. It only takes one touch of a Chieftain and you are soon filthy again. Later, time is spent searching for dead wood, and oil helps the bonfire blaze into the night. The squadron soon gathers with beer in hand. It doesn't take long for Wolfgang's chip wagon to arrive. How does he find us every time?

Armoured Fighting Vehicles of the Regiment

by Staff-Sergeant J A Dyer
Motor Transport Officer

From mechanisation to amalgamation the types of armoured fighting vehicles used by the 3rd and 7th Hussars were varied to say the least. Initially there were not enough tanks to meet establishments and then, as re-armament got going, squadrons often had different equipments, with all the problems this involved. It was not until mid-1943 that both Regiments were organised with just one main vehicle.

Both Regiments were equipped initially with Vickers Mk VI light tanks, with a crew of three and two machine guns, a .50 and a .303 inch. These were used in the early desert battles, the 3rd Hussars adding some captured Italian M13s mounting a 47 mm gun to their complement. Meanwhile, the 7th Hussars were being re-equipped with the A9/A10 Cruisers, to be followed by the better Crusader Mk I in early 1941. These tanks were armed with a 2 pdr gun and two Besa 7.92 mm machine guns.

In Burma the 7th Hussars used the American M3 Stuart light tank, known as the "Honey", with a 37 mm main armament. Meanwhile, the 3rd Hussars were equipped successively with the American M3, the 75 mm Sherman, the Grant with a 75 mm in a sponson and a 37 mm in a turret, and finally the British Crusader Mk III mounting a 6 pdr gun. By the Italian campaign both Regiments were equipped with Shermans. Towards the closing stages the 3rd Hussars had DD (Duplex Drive) Valentines, but they were not used in action. On the other hand, the 7th Hussars DD Shermans were.

In Palestine the 3rd Hussars had American Staghound armoured cars, while in Italy after the war the 7th Hussars had Crocodiles, the Churchill flame-throwing tank and trailer. Both Regiments became divisional anti-tank regiments for a time, having variously the 75 mm Cromwell, the 77 mm Comet and the American M10, mounting a 17 pdr in an open turret.

Before amalgamation the Centurion was introduced and was the main fighting vehicle of the early 1960s, the series ending with the formidable Mk XIII with its 105 mm gun. In 1967 a role change led to the Saladin armoured and Ferret scout cars becoming the standard equipment. Finally, the Regiment was equipped with the 120 mm Chieftain which, in a much improved version, is in service today.

In this short account it has not been possible to list the recce vehicles or the many variants issued at one time or another.

CHAPTER EIGHT

Some Unusual Facts

In the 1690s a Dragoon's horse had not to exceed 15 hands. They had to carry 18 stone in full marching order. This was later increased to 15.2 and 22 stone.

In 1695 the strength of the 3rd Hussars was 657 all ranks. The cost of upkeep in that year was £20,652–18s–4d.

Alexander Cannon, second Colonel of the 3rd Hussars, remained loyal to King James II when the Commanding Officer and most of the Regiment went over, with almost all of the rest of the Army, to King William. It was a terrible time of divided loyalties. Subsequently, Cannon took over command of the now-rebel Jacobite Forces when Dundee was killed at the Battle of Killiecrankie, 1689, in the moment of victory.

The establishment for a Regiment of Dragoons in 1690 was 31 officers and 354 other ranks. It was based on six Troops, each of one captain, one lieutenant, one cornet, two sergeants, three corporals, two drummers, two hautboys, and fifty "private dragoons". In 1694 Cunningham's Dragoons (later the 7th Hussars) were brought to War Establishment by the addition of two extra Troops and increasing all eight Troops to sixty "private dragoons".

In theory in the 1690s both the Colonel and the Lieutenant Colonel commanded Troops; in practice it was left to the Captains. However both of them received double pay: for their rank and the Troop.

In 1729 King George II ruled that a Dragoon recruit should be at least 5 feet 10 inches in his "stockings".

In 1748 two Troops of Honeywood's Dragoons (7th Hussars) were stationed in Birmingham.

By 1751 all regiments were numbered and in that year the use of the Colonels' names in the titles was expressly forbidden.

The supply of boots in the Warburg campaign of 1760 ran out. The 7th Hussars, covering their feet with straw, earned the nickname "Strawboots".

The summer of 1782 in Southern England must have been exceptional: "All parades of Troops and Squads are to be in the Shade as it is highly Prejudicial to the Health of the Men being Exposed to long in the Sun during the present intense heat".

7TH HUSSARS' DAILY ORDERS SALISBURY 19 JUNE 1782

During the 19th Century there were numerous instructions on the subject of facial hair, applying equally to officers and men. From 1812, hussars were required to wear moustaches, while dragoons had to shave the upper lip. After 1841, moustaches became general for all cavalrymen.

"From the great proportion of leisure hours which occur in a military life, the profession of arms has generally been stigmatized as an idle one, and indeed if it be considered abstractedly with reference only to garrison and regimental duties and independently of occasional service abroad, there is certainly no profession which in the ordinary pursuit of it enforces less actual study or personal exertion. The imputation of idleness however can attach upon such officers alone as enter the army with no other view than as an amusement, or upon such as have neither principle nor honour to influence, nor energy to excite them to the performance of the many important functions, they are called upon in duty to their King and Country to fulfil."

THE OPENING PARAGRAPH OF THE PREFACE STANDING ORDERS FOR THE THIRD OR KING'S OWN REGIMENT OF DRAGOONS, 1804

In 1818 the 3rd Regiment of Dragoons bitterly resented being converted to Light Dragoons. The Duke of York explained that "a much larger body of heavy than of light" cavalry would be "particularly injurious to the British army" when light cavalry were needed in the "colonial possessions".

In June 1838 in India on training 2 officers and 73 troopers of the 3rd Hussars died of "heat apoplexy".

During the summer of 1855 the 3rd Hussars travelled by train from Manchester to London – the first recorded occasion as far as is known.

In 1879 the 3rd Hussars left India, having been in the Mhow cavalry barracks for nearly seven years. The barrack damages amounted only to the trifling sum of 42 rupees 11 annas.

Although there had been a trial reorganisation in 1869, it was not until 1892 that the Squadron became more than a temporary tactical grouping of Troops.

In 1942 only one 7th Hussar tank – a Honey – survived to come out of Burma. Turretless, it became the command tank of the 7th Indian Light Cavalry and, with the startling name of "The Curse of Scotland", it re-entered Rangoon in 1945 with the XIVth Army.

The two War Memorials which commemorate those killed in the Second World War are the Flag Pole (3rd Hussars, 195 killed) and Statue (7th Hussars, 140 killed). Both memorials are saluted. The Brass Gong commemorates the 193 3rd Hussars killed in the First World War.

CHAPTER NINE

Colonels and Commanding Officers since Amalgamation

COLONELS OF THE REGIMENT:

Major General R Younger CB CBE DSO MC DL	3 Nov 1958–3 Nov 1961
Colonel Sir Douglas Scott Bt	3 Nov 1961–17 Aug 1965
Brigadier D H Davies MC	17 Aug 1965–15 Aug 1969
General Sir Patrick Howard-Dobson GCB ADC Gen	15 Aug 1969–1 Jun 1975
Colonel M Fox MC	1 Jun 1975–1 Jun 1981
Lieutenant General Sir Robin Carnegie KCB OBE	1 Jun 1981–

COMMANDING OFFICERS OF THE REGIMENT:

Lieutenant Colonel D B Wormald DSO MC	3 Nov 1958–1 Dec 1958
Lieutenant Colonel D H Davies MC	1 Dec 1958–20 Feb 1961
Lieutenant Colonel M Fox MC	20 Feb 1961–13 Sep 1963
Lieutenant Colonel P J Howard-Dobson	13 Sep 1963–29 Sep 1965
Lieutenant Colonel A M L Hogge	29 Sep 1965–29 Sep 1967
Lieutenant Colonel R M Carnegie OBE	29 Sep 1967–11 Aug 1969
Lieutenant Colonel M B Pritchard	11 Aug 1969–20 Nov 1971
Lieutenant Colonel J B Venner MC	20 Nov 1971–6 May 1974
Lieutenant Colonel J W F Rucker	6 May 1974–18 Nov 1976
Lieutenant Colonel R D H H Greenwood	18 Nov 1976–26 Apr 1979
Lieutenant Colonel H M Sandars	26 Apr 1979–7 Feb 1982
Lieutenant Colonel J J J Phipps	8 Feb 1982–18 Jul 1984
Lieutenant Colonel D J M Jenkins	19 Jul 1984–

Bibliography

1. There are two excellent books which take the history from the raising of the Regiments to amalgamation:
    The Galloping Third, Hector Bolitho, JOHN MURRAY, 1963
    The 7th Queen's Own Hussars, J M Brereton, LEO COOPER, 1975

2. There are four books which cover specific periods:
    The 3rd (King's Own) Hussars 1914–1919, H T Willcox, JOHN MURRAY, 1925
    The 7th (Queen's Own) Hussars (2 Vols.), C R B Barrett, R.U.S.I., 1914
    The Years Between: 7H 1911–1937, Roger Evans, GALE AND POLDEN, 1965
    The Seventh and Three Enemies, George Davy, HEFFER, 1952

3. There are three interesting 19th century books:
    The Standing Orders of the 3rd Dragoons, DUBLIN, 1804
    Historical Record of the 3rd Light Dragoons, Richard Cannon, PARKER, 1847
    Historical Record of the 7th Hussars, Richard Cannon, PARKER, 1842

4. The definitive study on British Cavalry 1816–1919 is:
    A History of the British Cavalry 1816–1919 (4 Vols.– 3 already published), The Marquess of Anglesey, LEO COOPER, 1973

5. Since the 1920s, many short histories, standing orders, etc, have been published. Copies of these are held at Home Headquarters, along with an extensive reference library and a list of all books known to contain chapters or references of regimental interest.

The British Reinforced Concrete Engineering Co. Ltd, without whom this book would not have been possible, are suppliers of all types of reinforcement and weldmesh for general purposes, and all types of fencing including security fencing.